The
Teacher's
Devotional

D0062583

The
Teacher's
Devotional

Copyright © CWR 2014. Published by CWR, Waverley Abbey House, Waverley Lane, Farnham, Surrey GU9 8EP, UK. Tel: 01252 784700 Email: mail@cwr.org.uk Registered Charity No. 294387. Registered Limited Company No. 1990308.

Printed in the UK by Linney Group.
ISBN: 978-1-78259-205-1

Contents

Contributors:
Carol Herzig (CH), Elaine Waddington (EW),
Rebecca Parkinson (RP), Helen Simpson (HS).

Meet the teachers

Carol Herzig began her teaching career as a Modern Languages teacher at a Norfolk secondary school, only resigning to follow God's call to overseas mission, where she met her husband, Andrew. Newly married, Carol then worked using her languages in business, before deciding in 2000 to return to the world of education. Carol went on to help set up, and then administer, a Victorian Schoolroom, in which she taught a full Victorian school day to visiting classes. She has subsequently worked for a Christian youth charity, the Matrix Trust; and for six years as an editor and writer for CWR. Carol's career has finally come full circle: she is again using her languages – this time in a primary school.

Elaine Waddington began her teaching career in Surrey and London, followed by sixteen years in the Middle East. She has taught students from many different backgrounds aged eight through to eighteen, enjoying the arts most of all, especially literature and poetry. One of the joys of living and working in the Middle East was having the opportunity to see the world through the eyes of others. And one of the challenges was attempting to learn Arabic! She now works at the Diocese of Guildford and in her non-work time enjoys leading quiet days and retreats and doing one-to-one spiritual accompaniment.

Rebecca Parkinson lives in Lancashire with her husband and their two children. Since graduating from Nottingham and Manchester Universities, Rebecca has worked as a teacher, science teacher adviser and university lecturer. She is also the author of a number of children's books, including the popular *Precious Princess* and *Harry's Hideout* series (CWR). Along with her husband, Rebecca leads the youth and children's work in a local church. In her spare time she enjoys any type of sport, especially netball, badminton, kayaking and other outdoor pursuits.

Helen Simpson has been an RE teacher in inner city London since 1986, after studying Theology at Manchester University. Undertaking a Masters degree with Chichester University enabled her to pursue further academic study in the field of education, which contributes to her work in the classroom and beyond. And as an experienced teacher of RE, she has contributed to the work of three London SACREs. She participates fully in the life of her church and enjoys taking part in retreats. She is particularly interested in the spiritual needs of those affected by dementia.

Jesus says,
'Come with me by yourselves to a quiet
place and get some rest.'
(Mark 6:31)

In His image

Genesis 1:26–31
'Then God said, "Let us make mankind in our image, in our likeness"' (v26)

We begin these notes with a very familiar passage – the implications of which are mind-blowing. We, and those we teach, are made in God's image. Whatever their appearance and behaviour, God has endued each person with a priceless dignity and worth; we bear *His* image.

God the Father sent His only Son, Jesus, to live as one of us (John 1:14). He subsequently gave us His Spirit to indwell us constantly. We are not then simply created 'in God's image' (which we'll consider again tomorrow), but He can also fully empathise with our humanity. What's more, the life, character and Spirit of God, indwelling in us as Christians, can touch those with whom we're in daily contact. So, in our week of readings entitled 'Roll call', we'll explore several names and characteristics of God (whose image we bear and whose life we carry); and look at how we can express His life and character in our varied roles as teachers.

A young teacher recently confided: 'I can only do so much for the children before they have to go home – I can't ensure they eat the right kinds of foods and have enough sleep, nor can I read them a bedtime story ...' Yet she does all she can to nurture and value each child, while in her care. Jesus often expressed His love for children. In His parable of the sheep and the goats, He declares: 'Truly I tell you, whatever you did for one of the least of these brothers and sisters of mine, you did for me' (Matt. 25:40). Although the strictest interpretation of 'these brothers and sisters' is those in the body of Christ, may they not also include the children we teach?

> **Lord, as I look into the faces of those I teach, help me know that as I love and serve them today I am also loving and serving You. Amen.**

Creator God

> **Genesis 1:26–28; Ephesians 1:15–2:10**
> *'So God created mankind in his own image, in the image of God he created them; male and female he created them.'*
> *(Gen. 1:27)*

We continue today looking at our theme of what it means to be 'made in the image of God'; a subject theologians have debated for centuries. I'd like to can offer my own testimony.

As a teacher in my twenties, I read Josh McDowell's book, *His Image, My Image*. The endorsements spoke of the book's 'life-changing' impact – and so it proved. As a teenager I'd taken on board negative comments: 'You have no common sense. You're not practical!' And, perhaps, worse still: 'You're not creative.' This book challenged every assumption and, in fact, outright lie I'd believed about myself. 'God is surely practical – He made the world, with all its intricacy and mechanical genius. God is the Creator of all – the source of all creativity. I'm made in His image – how can there not be an ounce of practicality or creativity in me?!' As I chose to believe differently about myself,

I began to discover new talents, both practical and creative, vital for my life and work. I'm so grateful for discovering those truths.

Where do you feel inadequate in your current professional or home life? Is what you're believing based on God's truth about yourself and your position in Christ, or have you, in fact, believed lies or exaggerated words of criticism? The apostle Paul writes: 'For we are God's handiwork, created in Christ Jesus to do good works, which God prepared in advance for us to do' (Eph. 2:10). The word translated 'handiwork' is the Greek *poiema*, which also means 'masterpiece'. Do not undervalue yourself, or your gifting – and where you lack, ask for God's supply. You are God's masterpiece.

> **Father God, may I draw on every resource and gift You have given me in Christ, to do the work You have called me to do. Amen.**

Prince of Peace

Isaiah 9:6–7; John 14:27
'*For to us a child is born … And he will be called Wonderful Counsellor, Mighty God, Everlasting Father, Prince of Peace.*'
(Isa. 9:6)

Writing these notes during Advent, I'm reminded of the wonderful names of God in this familiar verse from Isaiah. One I particularly love is 'Prince of Peace'. The Hebrew word *shalom* used here means so much more than our translation of 'peace'. Not only does it encompass safety, peace, wellbeing and welfare; but also health, prosperity, rest, wholeness and integrity. Jesus promises to give us this *shalom*, telling us not to let our hearts be troubled and fearful (John 14:27). We also carry this *shalom*, by His presence within us, and can share it with others.

School is often not a peaceful place to be. In addition to the normal disagreements children have, they bring with them their fears and frustrations from home, frequently outworked in their classroom behaviour. My friend, Edna, taught Religious Studies throughout the school and found the behaviour of certain towering, aggressive and rude Year 11 boys the most difficult to handle. She began to spend time every morning, before school, praying over the lintel of the classroom door that the Holy Spirit would fall on the pupils as they entered her room. Edna then prayed over each desk, that the Lord would speak into the heart of each child and meet their need, giving them peace. She continued this for weeks.

Change wasn't instant, but gradual. Edna began to sense that while those pupils were in her room their hearts were being touched. A few months later, the same Year 11 boys, no longer rude to her, commented that her classroom was the most peaceful place in the school. They felt safe there.

> **Whatever you may be facing today, may God's *shalom* peace invade your heart and touch those you meet through His presence within you.**

The Good Shepherd

Psalm 23:1–6; John 10:1–15

'The LORD is my shepherd, I lack nothing.
He makes me lie down in green pastures,
he leads me beside quiet waters'
(Psa. 23:1–2)

We may all have taught a child with so much potential who, through distraction, discouragement or being led astray, eventually gives up. For me, it was 'Tom'. One of the most gifted in the class, he enjoyed French. But over time, as peers led him into trouble, he gave up on school. I battled on, trying to pull him back ... and he hated me for it. Why did I bother? Was it for him or for me? But 'Tom' got his pass (the only one) – and years later thanked me profusely.

Jesus tells a parable, in Luke 15, of the shepherd who spends time and energy going after that one hundredth 'lost sheep'. He tells us too that He is our shepherd, the 'Good Shepherd' of the flock, who knows each of us, His sheep, individually and is known by us.

The imagery of the shepherd runs throughout the Old Testament. In his famous psalm, David talks of God's care of him through every season of life. The Lord knows when he is facing fears that threaten to overwhelm him; when he is reaching exhaustion and needs rest, nourishment and restoration.

We are 'shepherds' to the flock of children God has given us to care for – and this role is so key that it will be considered further in a later week. Caring for that hundredth sheep, especially, time and time again, is draining, frustrating and emotionally exhausting. But do we allow our 'Good Shepherd' to tend us too? Do we listen when He tells *us* to stop and rest: to take extra time out to feed and be replenished spiritually, emotionally and physically? Our Good Shepherd promises to feed and restore us. Let's ask for His daily help and renewal as we tend our own flock.

> **Lord, You are my shepherd. Help me to listen to Your voice and draw on Your wisdom, especially when caring for 'the hundredth sheep'. Amen.**

Immanuel

Matthew 28:16–20
*'And surely I am with you always,
to the very end of the age.' (v20)*

Marilyn Monroe once famously said in a film: 'It's a terrible thing to be lonesome, especially in the middle of a crowd.' Similarly, loneliness, isolation or feeling 'on your own' can be a real problem for teachers.

One beautiful name of God is 'Immanuel', meaning 'God with us' (Isa. 7:14; Matt. 1:23). In the wilderness, a visible sign of God's abiding presence accompanied the people of Israel: a pillar of cloud by day and of fire by night (Exod. 13:21–22). Centuries later, King David wrote: 'Where can I flee from your presence? If I go up to the heavens, you are there; if I make my bed in the depths, you are there' (Psa. 139:7–8). And Jesus promised to be with His disciples always (Matt. 28:20), saying: 'the Father ... will give you another advocate to help you and be with you for ever – the Spirit of truth' (John 14:16–17). So the truth is: we are not alone in the classroom – Immanuel God *is* with us.

For several years I taught visiting classes in a Victorian Schoolroom. I felt intimidated being scrutinised by onlookers from the back row (sometimes the Head, the class teacher, a teaching assistant and several parents). I felt God say, 'Before they arrive, visualise Jesus sitting on the back row, smiling at you. He is with you'. Making myself aware of God's presence in that room made a huge difference. A friend said that whenever she glanced at the classroom clock she was reminded of God's presence with her.

What is it for you? How can you become more aware, every day, of God's loving presence? The Lord God, Immanuel, is with you. You are not alone.

> **Lord, when I lack confidence and You seem far away, please remind me that You are with me. Amen.**

Wonderful Counsellor

John 14:15–31

‘ *'I will ask the Father, and he will give you
another advocate to help you and be with
you for ever' (v16)* ’

A nother of my favourite names of God, taken
from Isaiah 9:6, is 'Wonderful Counsellor' –
a title that applies especially to the Holy Spirit.
As we read Jesus' words today, He promises to send
His disciples that same 'Counsellor to be with [them]
for ever – the Spirit of truth' (vv16–17, NIV 1984).
The Greek word *parakletos*, used in this passage to
describe the Holy Spirit (vv16,26), literally means
'comforter, advocate', or as J.B. Phillips powerfully
translates, 'the one who is coming to stand by you'.

Did you end this week aware of God's loving
approval or with criticism ringing in your ears?
(Satan will often find others to discourage us, or
we can be overly self-critical or tempted to believe
the lies about ourselves he may have fed us over
the years.) George Adams wrote, 'Encouragement
is oxygen to the soul'. In a culture often so negative
and discouraging, we need that oxygen daily.

So Jesus' gift of the Holy Spirit to us is vital as an indwelling, personal God-presence whose very character is to comfort, console, exhort, help, intercede, encourage and counsel. Are you asking Him every day to refill you with His life?

Jesus does not leave us alone. His presence, by the Holy Spirit, is with us, to indwell us, encourage us and stand by us. Whether you feel like Daniel's friends, about to enter a fiery furnace (see Dan. 3, especially vv24–25), or are looking forward to the coming week, or anything in between, take heart. The Holy Spirit, the great encourager, is interceding for you and will stand by you.

> **Holy Spirit, please refresh and refill me every day, that I may know the power of Your encouragement – and then encourage those I meet and teach. Amen.**

Teachers of joy

John 15:9–17

'*I have told you this so that my joy may be in you and that your joy may be complete.*'
(v11)

This week we are looking at the theme of joy. And I hope it's going to be a kind of 'hunt' for joy. In our workplaces, in our homes and daily lives – where might joy be lurking? And how do we make that joy our own? And perhaps, the key to it all – where does that joy actually come from?

Children have much to teach us about joy. For over twenty years I have taught both in this country and in the Middle East. Some of my examples over the next few days are drawn from this time, when truly the children and the older students became my teachers.

Another of my teachers has been C.S. Lewis, particularly through his *Chronicles of Narnia* books. This will come as no surprise to anyone who has read them. Lewis manages to transport us, adult and child reader alike, into a world of delights where conflict is often central, but never gets the last word.

We become as little children as we encounter Aslan. And, if we allow him, Aslan will lead us to the true giver of joy – Jesus.

And it is Jesus, Word of God encountered in the Scriptures, who reveals God's joy to us. It is He who shows us the joy of loving and serving God and one another. When speaking to the disciples about remaining in God's love, Jesus says those familiar words, 'I have told you this so that my joy may be in you and that your joy may be complete' (John 15:11).

We have a joyful God who wants to teach us what is at the heart of joy.

> **Lord, please teach me about Your joy – the joy of the Trinity that flows between Father, Son and Holy Spirit. The joy that You want to share with me. Amen.**

A God of joy?

Proverbs 8:22–31

'*Then I was constantly at his side. I was filled with delight day after day, rejoicing always in his presence, rejoicing in his whole world and delighting in the human race.*'
(vv30–31)

As we consider joy and the joy-filled life, one of the stumbling blocks we often find within ourselves is the question, 'But *is* God really a God of joy?' Life events, circumstances, other people's attitudes, and our own inner self sometimes shape our image of God, rather than the picture of God that is revealed in Jesus.

Today's verses from Proverbs paint a wonderful picture of Father and Son together at creation. It builds up to a glorious crescendo as they express their joy and delight in the masterpiece they have made. It is an echo of the account in Genesis 1 where every day 'God saw that it was good'. And on the final day 'God saw all that he had made, and it was *very* good' (Gen. 1:31, my italics).

Commentators such as Matthew Henry have no

doubt that this 'wisdom', the craftsman at God's side, is referring to Jesus. He is spoken of in the Gospel of John as the Word who was with God, 'In the beginning' (John 1:1).

Joy, delight and a sense of goodness are what characterise Father and Son as they work together on creation (and that includes creating you and me).

Allow these words from Proverbs to refresh your thinking about God. Read them over again, allowing the delight in the verses to speak to you.

> **Lord, thank You that You are a God who is full of joy. I want this truth to touch my mind and heart and my deepest self today. Amen.**

Childlike wonder

Matthew 18:1–5

'*unless you change and become like little children, you will never enter the kingdom of heaven.' (v3)*

As a primary school teacher I found that the most exciting time in the school calendar was the lead up to Christmas. Of course, it could also be the most stressful – the preparation, the plays, making decorations, lingering illness and perhaps even the threat of an Ofsted inspection. But the joy and anticipation of the children seemed somehow bigger than all this.

I taught for some years in a little co-operative school in the Middle East. Every first of December we teachers would assemble a simple nativity scene in the hallway. The Mexican clay figures were white and black with gold haloes and all of them knelt inside a rough, customised cardboard box with straw at the bottom. To finish it off, we placed a small tea light at the back of the stable – no health and safety here!

School started at eight o'clock and the most special moment was when the six-year-olds came in and caught their first sight of the nativity scene. Their most common reaction was to drop what they were carrying and rush up to the cardboard box, eyes fixed on the figures. It was just at their eye level. And then, a brave one or two would turn around to one of the teachers and whisper, 'Can we touch them?'

Their awe and joy at something so simple was a delight to behold. And Jesus invites us to approach life in this way too – 'unless you become like little children, you will never enter the kingdom of heaven' (v3).

> **Lord, teach me afresh how to approach You as a child – to shake off my cynicism and to learn again that sense of awe, delight and joy in the simplest of things. Amen.**

God's joy over us

Zephaniah 3:14–20

'*Be glad and rejoice with all your heart
... never again will you fear any harm ...
The LORD your God is with you, the Mighty
Warrior who saves. He will take great
delight in you; in his love he will no longer
rebuke you, but will rejoice over you with
singing.' (vv14–15,17)*

Another stumbling block, as we consider the theme of joy, is how we view ourselves. Much has been written by psychologists and counsellors in recent years about self-image, so much that we can be over familiar with the concept and so discount it as we reflect on our relationship with God. Or we think that we have dealt with issues of poor self-image. But it seems to be a common thing that we feel unworthy of God's love and God's joy.

It may be that we need to draw near as children again and allow God to pour out His love and joy. To receive what He has to say about our value in His eyes and His joy over us.

Today, why not spend some time reflecting on this verse from Zephaniah? Perhaps in a few moments' quiet, repeat the verse over and over to yourself. Imagine God rejoicing over you with singing: 'I will rescue ... I will gather ... I will bring you home. I will give you honour and praise' (vv19–20).

Allow the delight of God to resonate with you and to speak truth to you. He loves you. Receive His joyful affirmation.

> **Lord, what a happy picture of You as a rejoicing, singing God. And Your song is for me and over me. Thank You. Amen.**

Comfort and joy

Isaiah 49:13

'Shout for joy, you heavens; rejoice, you earth; burst into song, you mountains! For the LORD comforts his people and will have compassion on his afflicted ones.' (v13)

I would like to have given today's reading the title 'Surprised by Joy' but our dear friend C.S. Lewis has already used that. He talks about joy in the context of suffering and I want to tell a story from my own life that is an example of this, in its own small way.

I loved my work in our small pioneering school in the Middle East. Out of the blue one year, one of my teenage students became very difficult. At first supportive, her parents decided that the root to all her problems stemmed from me. The next few months became emotionally exhausting and bewildering, dealing with difficulties in the classroom which spilled over into relationships with parents.

Evenings would often find me in tears, not knowing what to do. I had a real sense that Jesus was walking through this with me, but still it was a hard path.

One day in Social Studies, the younger group and I had been attempting to make a version of panpipes. Nobody could raise a tune. Another failure.

That evening, my phone rang and an excited voice yelled, 'Listen, Miss, listen!' Loud trilling noises attacked my ear down the phone line. 'It works, it works! I've made it work!'

Jacob, one of my more challenging but very creative students, had arrived home and had not rested until he had scraped and carved and drawn a tune out of his panpipes. And he wanted to share his joy with me! Loudly.

I laughed and laughed with tears running down my cheeks and could only say, 'Oh thank you, Jacob, thank you.'

Surprised by Jacob. By panpipes. By joy. Surprised by God.

> **Lord, thank You that You surprise us with Your joy when we need it most. And sometimes we don't even have to go looking for it. Amen.**

Full measure

John 17:1–19

'*I pray for them. I am not praying for the world, but for those you have given me, for they are yours. All I have is yours, and all you have is mine. And glory has come to me through them ... I am coming to you now, but I say these things while I am still in the world, so that they may have the full measure of my joy within them.*' (vv9,13)

This is Jesus' prayer for His disciples as He faces suffering and death. And Jesus, our great intercessor, prays this for us too. He prays for us to have the full measure of His joy in our lives.

Over the last few days we have considered some aspects of joy: the creative, life-giving joy of God, the way in which He rejoices and sings over us, how we are to become like little children and how He teaches us through the children and young people we serve – sometimes surprising us.

At the close of this week, you may like to return briefly to each reflection and identify which day spoke most deeply to you. Perhaps take some more time with that theme, pondering the words of God and what they stirred in you. Sit quietly with God and then respond out of your heart. It may be that you want to give thanks or sing your own song of joy to God. It may be that you find a deeper longing or prayer in your heart. Pour this out to God.

Our prayer today joins with the prayer of Jesus – that we will be full of His joy.

> **Lord, please reveal places in my heart where I long for more of You and Your joy. Thank You that this is Your prayer too. May Your will be done and Your kingdom come in me. Amen.**

Being a servant

Nehemiah 1
'I was cupbearer to the king.' (v11)

It is interesting that even in the opening paragraphs of this book, attention is not immediately focused on Nehemiah, but rather on the problem of the broken walls of Jerusalem. Maybe this is an early indication as to what it is that makes a good leader. We don't see a man of power seeking the limelight. In fact, if anything, we see what could be classed as weakness. When bad news arrives from home, Nehemiah sits down and weeps. Then, as he begins his prayer, Nehemiah uses the word 'servant' a total of eight times in five verses (vv6,7,8,10,11). It is no surprise therefore, as the first chapter closes, to discover that Nehemiah was himself a servant – the cupbearer to the king.

This first chapter may seem like an unusual place to begin a study about leadership! It is however where all good leaders will begin – at the place of servanthood. It is impossible to be a good leader if we are not willing firstly to serve other people. Maybe the greatest example of this is found in John 13 where

Jesus wraps a towel around His waist and begins to wash His disciples' dirty feet. As the Son of God performs the task of the lowest servant He says, 'I have set you an example that you should do as I have done for you' (13:15).

In Matthew 20 we see the mother of James and John asking that her sons be given an important position in the future. As part of His answer Jesus says, 'whoever wants to be great among you must be your servant ... just as the Son of Man did not come to be served, but to serve' (Matt. 20:26,28). In leadership there are times when we will have to sort out problems, make tough decisions, lead others forward into new initiatives, but all of it starts here – with the heart of a servant.

> **Lord, as You gave Yourself for other people, help us to give ourselves in service to You and to others. Amen.**

Being real ...
being honest

Nehemiah 2:1–10

'*I was very much afraid*' (v2)

How many of us feel we need to put on a good face – to always look like we are coping? People in leadership can be particularly good at this! Afraid to show any chink in their armour, afraid to show they are struggling, afraid that, if they show some weakness, then people will think less of them or even try to steal their position!

Yesterday we saw Nehemiah crying as he heard the news that Jerusalem still lay in ruins. In today's passage we see him appearing before the King, unable to keep a smile upon his face. In ancient courts in that region it was forbidden that anyone should be sad in the king's presence, to be so was a punishable offence. It is no wonder that Nehemiah was 'very much afraid'. And yet he had already prepared for this situation. In 1:11, we see Nehemiah praying that God would somehow work things out so that the king would act favourably towards him. Nehemiah was aware of his own inability to sort out the problem and knew he was totally dependent upon God.

Good leaders are aware of their own shortcomings. They are conscious that they cannot do everything by themselves. They need other people and, as with Nehemiah, Christian leaders are aware that they need God. It is not wrong to feel afraid as a leader; sometimes we have to make tough decisions and do things that are unpleasant or unpopular. We do however need to be honest enough to admit our weakness to ourselves and allow God to fill those areas where we are in particular need of help.

Read 1 Timothy 4:12. It's quite a daunting prospect for a leader to live up to – 'set an example for the believers in speech, in conduct, in love, in faith and in purity'! However, God is able to do far more than anything we ask or imagine if we allow Him the space in our lives.

Lord, thank You that even when we feel at our weakest, You are always strong. Amen.

Walking in prayer

Nehemiah 1:4–11; 2:1–4
'*Then I prayed to the God of heaven*' (2:4)

In 1:4, Nehemiah sits down and begins to weep; in 2:2, he stands trembling before the king. However, in both cases his immediate response is the same – he prays. In fact, as we read through the whole of the book of Nehemiah we see a man who prays in every situation. Prayer is a natural part of everyday life. When Nehemiah is insulted 4:3 – he prays; when he is under attack 4:9 – he prays; as the walls are rebuilt, as the book of the Law is read, as social reforms are made – he prays. Even when everything is completed, in the last verse of the book, Nehemiah prays, asking God to be pleased with what he has done.

If we are to be good leaders we need to see the importance of prayer. Not simply praying when we are in some kind of emergency, but walking in prayer, realising that, as God is constantly with us, every detail of our lives is important to Him and can be brought to Him. The encouragement in 1 Thessalonians 5:17 to 'pray continually' doesn't mean we have to pray all the time! Rather it means that as we walk through our lives with God we have a constant companion – we always have someone with whom to share fears, joys, problems and hopes at any point of any day.

To be a good leader we need to be able to recognise that we can't manage alone. Let's ask God each day to guide us in everything we do, in every decision we make, in every relationship we encounter. As we move through the day let's remember to include God as we ask Him to help us to lead in the way He would want.

> **Lord, thank You that You never leave us.**
> **Thank You that You love us to talk to You**
> **and that You are always there to listen.**
> **Amen.**

Action and motivation

Nehemiah 2:11–20
'*They replied, "Let us start rebuilding."*
So they began this good work.' (v18)

We have seen Nehemiah sad, afraid, praying, speaking to the king – now we see him in action! As leaders there is a time to move!

Nehemiah arrives in Jerusalem and waits three days before he sets out to look at the walls. We don't know how he occupied this time. Maybe he rested, maybe he looked up old friends or maybe he waited quietly, praying for wisdom. We do know that he told no one his real reason for being there (v12). Sometimes leadership can be a lonely place where we need to prayerfully consider matters ourselves before talking to a wider circle. As, under cover of darkness, Nehemiah sees the extent of Jerusalem's destruction, we read that, 'God had put in [his] heart' what he should do (v12).

Then Nehemiah gathers the people together. It would be easy at this point for Nehemiah to make the people feel guilty for not rebuilding the walls earlier or to order them to start building. However, alongside the suggestion that they build the walls together, Nehemiah also tells them the story of his return, explaining how King Artaxerxes listened to him and sent him to Jerusalem. Convinced that God is with them, the people rally together and in chapter 3 we see people of every profession pulling together to build. The people's enthusiasm is so great that the walls are rebuilt in fifty-two days (6:15)!

Being able to motivate others is essential in leadership. Demanding that people follow our lead will ultimately fail. Like Nehemiah we need to put time and effort into taking people along with us. It is interesting to note that Nehemiah works with the people. In chapter 4 he repeatedly says 'we' rather than 'they'. He is there alongside, working as hard, if not harder, than anyone else and thus gaining people's respect. As leaders, let's not ask others to do the things that we would not be willing to do ourselves.

> **Lord, help us to lead by example. Help us to motivate others as they see our care and consideration for them. Amen.**

Courage and care

Nehemiah 4

'*What are those feeble Jews doing? ...
Can they bring the stones back to life from
those heaps of rubble ...?*' (v2)

A s the walls of Jerusalem begin to take shape, the leaders in the surrounding areas begin to worry. Whilst Jerusalem has lain in ruins, the Jewish people were easy to control. Once the walls are rebuilt and the people have returned to the city, this control will be lessened. In their fear they begin to taunt Nehemiah and the people. All of us know that the childhood saying, 'Sticks and stones may break my bones but words will never hurt me!' is simply not true! Words do hurt and sometimes they can be more painful and their effects far more longstanding than a physical injury. Nehemiah's response in verse 4 is not to complain or even answer back, but to pray and lead by example. The result is that the people continued to work 'with all their heart' (v6).

When the angry words eventually lead to violent threats (v8), Nehemiah prepares the people (v16) by giving out weapons and positioning the people strategically, but he doesn't quit in fear. His eyes are fixed on the task in hand but his heart is also focused on the protection of the people. Consequently the building continues even though the opposition leaders continue with their frightening tactics and schemes.

Throughout the building of the wall, Nehemiah showed both courage and care, two attributes that all leaders need at some point. Being in leadership means that at times we will not be popular. Often we will face criticism; often we will feel hurt. However, like Nehemiah we need to keep focused on the wellbeing and protection of those in our care as we move forward towards our goals. People matter – let's ask God to give us wise plans; let's listen to His guidance and then courageously move forward with other people's welfare in mind.

> **Lord, help us to be good leaders. Help us to hear Your voice and move forward with what You want us to do. But help us to never lose sight of the needs of those around us. Amen.**

Integrity

'*When I heard their outcry and these charges, I was very angry.*' *(v6)*

We have already seen that when Nehemiah hears that the walls of Jerusalem are broken down and realises the suffering of the people left there, he sits down and cries. Now we see another side to this compassionate leader. We see him as a man of integrity – 'the quality of being honest and having strong moral principles' (Oxford Dictionary).

It seems that at the same time as the walls are being rebuilt there is also a famine in the land. As people become desperate for grain they are re-mortgaging their homes and fields. At the same time the nobles in the area are demanding greater taxes and the result is that the poor are suffering to such an extent that their daughters are being sold into slavery! No wonder Nehemiah describes himself as 'very angry'! In verse 7 we see Nehemiah taking the time to ponder the problem before going to the nobles and facing them with a few home truths. Faced with Nehemiah's words the nobles are speechless (v8), and they give back what they have taken and agree to make no more demands (v12). Quite a success!

As leaders we need to be people of integrity, standing against wrong and standing up for what is right, as well as for those in need. We also need to be gathering people of integrity around us. Nehemiah appoints a commander simply because 'he was a man of integrity and feared God more than most people do' (7:2) – not always a quality seen on an application form or noted at an interview!

Let's ask God to help us as leaders in this area. Let's ask Him that our judgments will not be clouded by fear or workplace politics, but that we will be 'honest and have strong moral principles'.

> **Lord, help me never to lose sight of what is right. Help me to find the strength to stand against wrongdoing and to always seek to help those in need. Amen.**

Our hearts have a home

Isaiah 49:8–18

'*Can a mother forget the baby at her breast and have no compassion on the child she has borne? Though she may forget, I will not forget you! See, I have engraved you on the palms of my hands' (vv15–16)*

'Teacher ... what must I do to inherit eternal life?' (Luke 10:25). In the time of Jesus, students showed their understanding by the questions they asked rather than the answer they gave in end of year assessments or examinations. This young man, encouraged by Jesus, answered his own question, using his knowledge of Scripture: 'Love the Lord your God with all your heart and with all your soul and with all your strength and with all your mind' (Luke 10:27).

This week we will explore the first: loving God with all your heart.

The key place to start in fulfilling this command is to know, truly and deeply, that God first loved us with all His heart. Today's key verse shows how close He keeps us to Him, how He would never forget us and how He made us to be in relationship with Him.

We are loved and known, and in return we must love God our Father with our whole being.

'Whoever has my commands and keeps them is the one who loves me. The one who loves me will be loved by my Father, and I too will love them and show myself to them' (John 14:21).

Perhaps take a moment at the beginning of this week to confess any ways in which you have strayed from God's commands and commit this week to acting in obedience and love in everything you do.

> **Dear Lord, help me to love You in all that I do today. Help me to express this heartfelt love through my emotions, and how I respond to others. Help me to channel my energy so that my strength is used to worship You in thought, word and action. Help me to use my intellect to think and focus fully on Your love for us all. Thank You loving God. Amen.**

Don't lose heart

Psalm 73

'*God is the strength of my heart and my portion for ever' (v26)*

In a system that is becoming driven by results we need to hold fast to the knowledge that each person we teach or work alongside is made in the image of God. The way we are and the way we build relationships touches them as people first. Teaching is a relational profession. As teachers, we make a difference to our students even before their levels are calculated or, for staff, before their performance is managed. Sometimes we may wonder if we make any difference at all. Perhaps it would be easier if we didn't care?

In today's reading we see the psalmist wondering whether it is all worth the effort: 'Surely in vain I have kept my heart pure' (v13). But he then takes time out before the Lord and renews his strength of heart. Each school has a pastoral system through which we recognise the needs of both students and staff. It may be more explicit that the pastoral system has a student focus but each school has a duty of care to the staff working within it too. Seek the Lord's help in remembering our duty of care to students and colleagues; believers and non-believers.

> **Dear Lord, help me to live more fully by faith. Help me not to lose heart. It is easy to feel downhearted in the face of the many challenges that I encounter. I must be fully engaged in what I do in school but remind me to also remember the unseen things that are eternal. Lord, help me to reflect the gospel values of love for You and love for my neighbour. In my interactions with students and colleagues let me be gentle and respectful. Let me not be afraid to use the still moments to listen to the silence, to listen for You and to be thankful. Amen.**

An anxious heart

Matthew 6:25–34

' *Look at the birds of the air; they do not sow or reap or store away in barns, and yet your heavenly Father feeds them. Are you not much more valuable than they? Can any one of you by worrying add a single hour to your life?' (vv26–27)*

We are often so preoccupied with what we have to do that we are not always able to hear other people properly. Sometimes it feels that it is easy to be irritable and annoyed rather than have our hearts in the right place. If only there were more hours in the day we wonder! It is so easy in many occupations to be distracted by anxiety, especially so in teaching. The deadlines we set ourselves and the demands we make on ourselves as teachers are sometimes unnecessary. In the same way the deadlines we are given and the demands made on us can easily frustrate or even paralyse the creativity that is so essential for the teacher. Creativity, flair and innovation all need time, and as teachers we need to find those moments in our work, rather than look for more time just to add more administrative tasks!

Worrying and being anxious will not give us any more time in the day and might make us miss the moments of rest or conversation when they occur. We must live in the moment and all that is required of each of us is faith, trust and hope. This has to be our theological lesson for every day.

'See how the flowers of the field grow. They do not labour or spin' (v28).

> **'God, give us grace to accept with serenity the things that cannot be changed, courage to change the things which should be changed, and the wisdom to distinguish one from the other.' Reinhold Niebuhr (1892–1971). Lord, let these words focus my thinking today so that I keep a healthy sense of perspective. Amen.**

A vulnerable heart

Proverbs 4

'*pay attention to what I say; turn your ear to my words. Do not let them out of your sight, keep them within your heart; for they are life to those who find them and health to one's whole body. Above all else, guard your heart, for everything you do flows from it.' (vv20–23)*

It is interesting to observe how lonely the role of a teacher can be. There are times when the learning experience we create is supported by other adults in an educational role and others when it is just us and a student or a group.

How easy it is to see our role as 'The Sage on the Stage' or 'The Guide on the Side' in terms of didactic teaching or a more facilitative approach. Both roles seem so easy to define, but then life gets in the way. We may be the lone adult choosing our role but it is always in the context of our students and their learning.

Many of our students are easy to get along with and we build positive relationships in an equally easy way. But, sometimes there are the few individuals who, somehow, build such a large and dominating portrait in our imaginings. We allow ourselves to become irritated or angry so quickly with these students. Sometimes we allow ourselves to blame them for everything that goes wrong, whether they deserve it or not. How can we guard our vulnerable heart so that we approach these students in a positive way, understanding their context and learning needs?

> **Oh Lord, any angry words or thoughts that have come into my heart today please help me to get into perspective. Let me make the situation right before the day ends. Help me if my pride seems to be an obstacle to doing what is right. I ask this prayer through the name of Jesus, my teacher. Amen.**

A forgiving heart

Matthew 6:9–15

'For if you forgive other people when they sin against you, your heavenly Father will also forgive you. But if you do not forgive others their sins, your Father will not forgive your sins.' (vv14–15)

I have often been surprised by a surge of anger when telling off a student. Sometimes the anger has nothing to do with me, it is the student who is full of anger and for some reason I pick up on it. If I am not careful to recognise and discharge that anger in a quick prayer, my own anger can spill out in an unhelpful way. In his letter to the Ephesians, Paul wrote, 'In your anger do not sin' (4:26). As teachers we have a duty to keep an open and clear heart each day. In my own work I find I need to consciously let go of yesterday's annoyances and start again. This is a key to refreshment. The alternative in holding on to that anger or annoyance means that a callousness or resentment can grow, which can affect our relationship with colleagues and students. When Jesus gave His disciples a model for praying He included the thought that we should – we must – forgive others in the same way that we would wish to be forgiven. How can you build this into your life as a teacher?

> **Dear Lord, help me to forgive in my heart the people who have offended or hurt me today. Let this forgiveness be from my heart and not just my mouth so that I am truly living more of the gospel message of Jesus.**
> **Do not let the resentment stay in me. Let me reflect the loving face of our Saviour in my encounters with others. Amen.**

Half-hearted?

'*A happy heart makes the face cheerful, but heartache crushes the spirit. The discerning heart seeks knowledge, but the mouth of a fool feeds on folly. All the days of the oppressed are wretched, but the cheerful heart has a continual feast.*' (vv13–15)

If I am just counting the lessons to the end of the day, to the next holiday or even counting the days to my retirement, I will not be loving the Lord today with all my heart. More likely, I will be loving Him half-heartedly. We know in our hearts that this is the day that the Lord has made and He is concerned about all of it – including my part in it. So let us rejoice and be glad! It is the Lord that we're serving with all our heart, no one else.

There are so many stories in Christian tradition of individuals who demonstrated in a most wholehearted way their love for the Lord. I have recently been studying the life of Oscar Romero with A Level students. In the film *Romero* we were able to consider the life of a man who lived his life to the full, knowing the risks it entailed, but certain of the promise of Jesus Christ. Romero once said, 'A bishop may die, but the Church of God, which is the people, will never die'.

> **Heavenly Father, help me love You more fully in all that I do today – from the time I get up until the time I go to back to sleep. Let my love for You show in the way I speak and behave towards other people. Let me listen with interest and concern when people need me. Help me to follow the example of Your dear Son, who loved all those that He came into contact with. Amen.**

The Lord is my shepherd

Psalm 23

'*The LORD is my shepherd, I lack nothing.*'
(v1)

The Bible makes more than 200 references to shepherds or shepherding. Sometimes these references are to specific people such as the shepherds who were told of Jesus' birth (Luke 2); sometimes they are used to describe kings (2 Sam. 5:2) or leaders (Jer. 23:1); sometimes they are used to describe characteristics of God. In Psalm 23 we see David describing God as his shepherd in a beautiful poem, which is probably one of the best known passages in the Bible.

Shepherds in Bible times had a number of roles. Firstly, they were responsible for leading the flock to fresh grass and still water where they could eat, drink and rest in peace. Secondly, they would protect the sheep from wild animals (see 1 Sam. 17:34–35), keeping watch through the hours of darkness (Luke 2:8). Thirdly, they would care for the sheep, taking them to safe pastures, counting them regularly to ensure that none were missing (Luke 15:1–7), and even carrying the weak lambs in their arms (Isa. 40:11).

As the youngest in the family it would have been David's job to tend the family sheep. For many years he would have fulfilled each of the above roles and it is easy to imagine him sitting on the mountainside writing this psalm as the realisation dawned on him that God had cared for him throughout his life in a similar way. In this psalm we see the perfect shepherd, the protector and provider whose presence dispels fear and ultimately brings joy.

As we look this week at a number of shepherds in the Bible and the lessons we can learn from them, there is no better place to start than to remind ourselves that the Lord is our shepherd – providing for us, protecting us and beside us in every situation – we lack nothing!

> **Lord, thank You for this description of You:**
> **'He tends his flock like a shepherd: he gathers**
> **the lambs in his arms and carries them close**
> **to his heart; he gently leads those that have**
> **young' (Isa. 40:11). Thank You for the way You**
> **care for us. Amen.**

The welcoming shepherd

1 Samuel 22:1–2

'*All those who were in distress or in debt or discontented gathered round him, and he became their commander' (v2)*

Following on from his killing of the Philistine giant Goliath, David is initially welcomed by Saul and given a high rank in the king's army (18:5). However, as David's popularity increases, jealousy quickly sets in and Saul begins to plan how to get rid of him. Eventually, David flees for his life to a cave at a place called Adullam.

Psalm 142 is written by David while he is in this cave. In the psalm he speaks of being 'in desperate need' and states that 'no one is concerned for me', and 'no one cares for my life'. You would imagine that into this situation God would send some kind of hero to help the future king. Instead a trickle of people begin to arrive at the cave (22:2), all of them with problems, none of them the kind of people who would be a natural choice! Yet David works with these people until they become a mighty army that is feared by all the surrounding countries.

One of the dictionary definitions of shepherding is: 'One who cares for and guides a group of people'. In today's passage we see the start of this process for David as he welcomes the distressed and the discontented, seeing in them the potential that no one else has noticed. What a picture of a good teacher! Seeing the potential in children, caring for and guiding them; seeing what they can become or what they may achieve, even if at present no one else can see it. What a picture also of the way that God sees us! He accepts us with all our weaknesses and insecurities. He doesn't wait until we are at a required standard; He loves us as we are now.

> **Lord, You care for the distressed, those in debt, the discontented, the outcast. Help us to do the same, realising that each person is of great importance to You. Amen.**

The famous shepherds

Luke 2:8–20

*'When they had seen him, they spread the
word concerning what had been told them
about this child' (v17)*

There are many well-known shepherds in the
Bible – Abraham, Isaac, Jacob, David ... but
today we think about the most famous of
biblical shepherds. Often seen on cards at Christmas
or appearing in nativity plays, these shepherds are
suddenly taken from their normal work in the fields to
the bedside of the Son of God! Quite a transformation!

In the time of Abraham, shepherding was seen
as a noble occupation but as time progressed, this
changed. By the time of Jesus' birth, shepherds were
considered to be of little importance. Many shepherds
lived outside the city walls, spending much of their
time in the fields, often travelling many miles to find
suitable pasture land. By the Pharisees and religious
teachers, shepherds were often seen as unclean due to
their work keeping them from observing the Sabbath
and their handling of the sheep compromising their
religious purity. These shepherds were definitely

in the group referred to as 'sinners' (Mark 2:16). From a social viewpoint, shepherds were considered to be of the lowest class. And yet it is these shepherds, out of all the people in Bethlehem that night, to whom hosts of angels appear! It is these shepherds that are the first to see Jesus, the promised Messiah!

Why? Surely because Jesus came for all people, of every race and every social class. In God's eyes there is no difference and He wanted to make this clear from the moment Jesus appeared in the world. What a challenge to us as teachers. No child is more or less important. Money, possessions, parental pressure, ability, social status – all of these make no difference to the importance of any child. Let's ask God to help us see all children through His eyes and to treat them all with equality.

> **Lord, help us to see people as You see them,**
> **without prejudice and always with love.**
> **Amen.**

The searching shepherd

Luke 15:1–7

'*Doesn't he leave the ninety-nine in the open country and go after the lost sheep until he finds it?*' (v4)

A t the end of each day the shepherd would count his sheep into the sheep fold. If the flock were grazing near home this fold would be a fixed square stone structure with one small door. If the shepherd had led the flock to distant pastures he would erect a similar make-shift fold from thorns and branches. Once the sheep were safely inside he would sleep in the doorway, thus protecting the flock from wild animals – the beasts would have to climb over the shepherd to gain access to the sheep. The implication in this beautiful passage is that, as the shepherd counts the sheep into the fold he realises that one is missing. To us this may seem insignificant; after all he still has 99 left! But to a shepherd, who knows his flock, this one sheep is vitally important. So out he goes into the darkness, searching until that one sheep is found.

Applying this to our role as teachers I believe this is where true shepherding begins – seeing the absolute value of a person and going out of our way to show that person that they really do matter. Imagine if this lost sheep had been able to think! He finds himself lost in the dark, frightened and unable to find his way home. Suddenly he hears his master's voice calling him and realises that he has come to find him. More than that, his master lifts him up and carries him back to his waiting family! How valued that sheep must have felt! No longer does he just feel like an unnoticed member of the crowd. He feels loved, noticed and wanted. We can all think of children who need to feel that way. What a privilege to 'find' them, lift them up and bring them into a place of safety.

What about us? We can often feel like this lost sheep. Maybe we need to remind ourselves today that we are precious enough for God to 'look' for us.

Lord, help us to notice the lost and the lonely. Amen.

The knowing shepherd

John 10:1–15
*'I am the good shepherd; I know my sheep
and my sheep know me' (v14)*

Having slept all night in the doorway of the sheepfold to protect his sheep, the shepherd would rise at dawn and call to his flock. Upon hearing their master's voice, the sheep would leave the safety of their fold, knowing that their master would not lead them into any danger. If a different shepherd were to call them, the sheep would stay inside the fold. The sheep knew the shepherd's voice in the same way as we need to know God's voice. But it is the phrase 'I know them' that gives us a clue to great shepherding.

During a recent visit to a dairy farm I was fascinated to find that the farmer had pet-names for most of his cows. To me they all looked similar – to him they were all individuals. As we read this passage we are drawn to a shepherd who knows his sheep. Phrases such as 'He calls [them] by name' (v3) and 'all his own' (v4), produce the picture of a shepherd who sees each sheep as an individual, and who cares deeply.

When Jesus describes Himself as the good shepherd we are pulled into an even more beautiful illustration – He knows His sheep – He knows us! Even better than that, despite the fact that He knows us with all our faults, in verse 15 He says 'I lay down my life for the sheep'! When Jesus spoke these words they were not initially understood (v6), but now we know they pointed to the cross, when Jesus would do exactly what He said – give His life for us. Surely we want to follow a shepherd who loved us so much.

As we seek to shepherd our children, do we know them and do they have any reason to 'follow' us? Do they know that we care?

> **'Greater love has no one than this: to lay down one's life for one's friends' (John 15:13). Thank You Lord, that You laid down Your life for me. Amen.**

The feeding shepherd

John 21:15–23
'Jesus said, "Feed my sheep"' (v17)

When Peter makes his 'I will lay down my life for you' statement at the Last Supper, within hours he has gone back on his promise and denied that he even knew Jesus. After the resurrection, as Jesus takes Peter for a walk along the beach, Peter no doubt realised there were things that needed to be said, issues that needed to be faced. However, Jesus' requests are unexpected! He asks Peter to do three things, each time broadening the brief of what it means to be a shepherd of people.

In Bible times, shepherds would often return to pastures near their home towns for the lambing season. Here they would be on hand to help with difficult births, aid lambs that were not suckling correctly and ensure that during the first few weeks of life, when the lambs couldn't fend for themselves, they were well fed. As the lambs grew, the shepherd was responsible for every part of their welfare: checking for disease, leading them to good pastures, protecting them, rescuing them, caring for the injured, providing water and food. As Jesus tells Peter to 'feed my lambs' and 'take care of my sheep', the level of commitment that Jesus is asking Peter to take on increases until, in His final statement, Jesus points out the enormity of the commitment that Peter is taking on. To truly feed and lead Jesus' followers would ultimately cost Peter his life.

Are we prepared for the cost of shepherding? To shepherd in the way the Bible suggests means commitment of time and energy. It may mean heartache; it won't always be easy but as we shepherd our children we know we have the good shepherd to guide us and, as we follow His example, we can play a vital part in our children's lives.

Lord, help us to shepherd our children well as we follow Your example in our lives. Amen.

A bad start to the day

Matthew 14:1–14
'When Jesus heard what had happened,
he withdrew by boat privately to a
solitary place.' (v13)

O ver the next week our theme is 'a day in the life of Jesus'. We're going to be walking through it with Him, seeing how He responds and reacts, how He deals with and even invites in the unexpected, the unwelcome, the demands and the miraculous. If you have time, try to read the whole chapter at the beginning of the week.

Jesus' day begins with some really bad news – word comes to Him that His cousin, John the Baptist, has been unjustly and cruelly murdered at the hands of Herod.

Since they were both in the womb, the two cousins' lives have been intertwined and each has pointed to the other as sent by God – one the forerunner and herald, the other, the Light, the Son of God.

John's death is crushing news to Jesus.

His immediate response is to find some solitude, to get away from everyone and to deal with this news alone. His desire to be alone is emphasised by the words chosen: 'withdrew', 'privately', 'solitary' (v13).

Sometimes, when we read verses like this about Jesus, we gloss over them. We rush on to the next verses where He seems to rally Himself and throws Himself into the work of the day. And we say to ourselves, 'That's what I must do: get over it'.

Jesus' initial response was not to 'get over it' with activity, but to withdraw to be with His Father and to be with His sorrow. He recognises the significance of this moment and wants to make room to reflect and to pray.

> **Lord, thank You that You know what it is
> to have a bad start to the day, to receive
> bad news. Thank You that Your life was not
> without the unexpected or the unwelcome.
> Teach me to turn aside with You to the
> Father when I find myself in that place.
> Amen.**

Pressures build

Matthew 14:13–15

' *'the crowds followed him on foot from the towns. When Jesus landed and saw a large crowd, he had compassion on them and healed those who were ill.' (vv13–14)* '

Yesterday, we left Jesus withdrawing by boat to a solitary place. But it wasn't solitary for long. The crowds, perhaps using some ancient form of Twitter, find where He is and simply turn up. Thousands of them. A flash mob, clamouring for His attention.

Does Jesus turn the boat around and head for another quieter part of the shore or even the middle of the lake? No, He lands the boat and seeing them has 'compassion on them'. He is moved to help them. And He does, reaching out, moving among them, bringing the healing of God.

What is so intriguing about these verses is that we see Jesus responding to exactly the same kind of pressures we have as we enter the classroom daily. Like Jesus, we may have personal or work-related issues that need our attention, that preoccupy us, but somehow God enables us to reach beyond ourselves and draw on His compassion. Both for ourselves and for those in our care.

As we read on in this chapter, we see that actually Jesus is holding on to that need for solitude and He will return to it later. He seems to tuck it away somewhere so that He can attend to the matters of the day, drawing on God's strength when He is 'in the thick of it'.

> **Lord, when life and work is clamouring for my attention please draw me into that place of compassion where I will find You, helping me to love and teach and heal. Amen.**

Bread and more bread

Matthew 14:15–21
'*Jesus replied, "They do not need to go away. You give them something to eat."*'
(v16)

The evening comes, Jesus has been with the crowds all day and His weary disciples ask Him to send all the people home. Just as they think this busy day is over, Jesus ratchets up the pressure: 'You give them something to eat' (v16).

Are the disciples being a little sarcastic when they answer Him by offering the five loaves and the two fish? Or are they simply offering Him the facts and seeing what He will make of them? If only we could put ourselves in the shoes of the disciples, being in the story afresh without knowing the ending!

I cannot read this scene without thinking of *The Life of Christ,* an outdoor modern passion play that takes place every year at the Wintershall estate in Surrey. The audience sits on the grass alongside the actors, becoming part of the story. It is such a joyful moment when the bread begins to miraculously multiply in Jesus' hands. The disciples bound around the crowd, handing out loaves of bread, huge grins on their faces. And the audience responds with wide smiles and shouts of 'Over here!'

What joy and surprise there is when we are suddenly caught up in something unexpected that God is doing. Like the disciples, we might have been winding up our service for the day, and then something remarkable happens …

> **Lord, I want to be in on all that You're doing and the joy that You bring. May I never grow tired of working alongside You. Give me a fresh bounce in my step and in my heart as I serve You. Amen.**

Alone to pray

Matthew 14:22–24

'he went up on a mountainside by himself to pray. Later that night, he was there alone' (v23)

A t the very end of the day, Jesus sends the crowds home and tells the disciples to cross the lake in the boat. He turns His attention to what He planned to do at the beginning of the day – He makes His way alone into the hills to pray.

We are not told what He prayed or how, but His heart is set on being alone with the Father. Perhaps now He returns to the earlier news about John, lifting His sadness before the Father. Maybe, He also talks over the rest of the day – the crowds, the healings, the bread and fish. And in the quiet, does He listen for the still, small voice of His Father?

Often in the Gospel accounts we read of Jesus alone with the Father, praying. Some of the recorded prayers have echoes of the Psalms. And some are fresh and new, like the one we have come to know as the Lord's prayer.

What is clear is that Jesus' relationship with His Father, forged in the solitary places, is the hub of all His activity. Jesus is drawn into His Father's presence, sensing the pull like the undertow of the ocean. And from this certain, sure place He is able to give of Himself all day.

Let's look for that quiet place in our own days wherever we can find it – before school, between classes, in the quietness of the classroom at the end of the day. God waits for us.

> **Lord, draw me into Your presence. Bring me to that place of stillness where I can pour out my heart and hear Your voice. Amen.**

What was all that about?

Matthew 14:23–27
'Jesus went out to them, walking on the lake.' (v25)

The disciples are out in the boat, which is being buffeted about by the wind and the waves as they try to cross the lake. What comes next is extraordinary. Jesus finishes His prayer and simply steps onto the water and makes His way towards the boat.

Our theologians tell us that this is all about Jesus being Lord of creation; after all, He is the ruler of all that He has made. But what a strange thing to do! I have often wondered if Jesus was so preoccupied with His day and His thoughts that He stepped from land onto sea, not even noticing the difference. And scaring the disciples silly into the bargain!

When I read a passage like this, I am very aware of the 'otherness' of Jesus, that although He is fully man, He is also fully God; a God not always easy to understand, difficult to decipher. Some of His ways are very different from ours.

Do you ever ask with genuine curiosity, 'What was that all about?'

If we allow them, children and young people often ask the really searching questions – some that even the theologians cannot answer. Encourage those you teach to ask the difficult questions. Ask difficult questions yourself. And let's not be afraid of this wonderful conundrum, Jesus. 'It is I. Don't be afraid' (v27), says Jesus.

'For my thoughts are not your thoughts, neither are your ways my ways' (Isa. 55:8).

> **Lord, indeed Your thoughts are not my**
> **thoughts and Your ways not my ways.**
> **Thank You that You are God – indescribable,**
> **uncontainable, sometimes puzzling,**
> **gloriously God. Amen.**

Reassuringly present

Matthew 14:28–36

' *'Jesus reached out his hand and caught him.' (v31)* '

We come to the final part of this day in Jesus' life. He walks towards the boat on the waves and Peter, spontaneous and irrepressible as always, wants to be part of what is going on. He steps into the water, takes a few steps and then begins to sink. Jesus reaches out, grabs him and pulls him into the boat.

"'You of little faith," he said, "why did you doubt?"' (v31).

We can read these words as if Jesus is angry with Peter. There is a film adaptation of the Gospel of Matthew where Jesus is portrayed as a warm, compassionate Messiah who laughs often. In this scene, He grabs Peter with both arms and helps him into the boat, chuckling and smiling.

This portrayal offers insight into how Jesus walks with us. He invites us into situations where there is an element of risk. He dares us to put our trust in God and not to be afraid of getting things wrong.

He corrects us, but not in anger. Like a master with an apprentice, or a teacher with a student.

And there are obvious parallels with our relationships with our students – walking alongside them, offering them not just knowledge but experiences where they will learn. Correcting them when necessary, but not in anger. They may fail (as we do) but we are beside them, reassuringly present, just as Jesus walks beside us.

This whole day with Jesus has been a true learning experience – like the disciples, we are called not simply to observe Jesus and take note, but to be involved in His work beside Him. To be 'in the thick of it' with Him.

> **Lord, I want to be a true disciple of Yours, an apprentice learning beside You, not afraid to take risks. And I want to learn how to walk with my students, bringing Your warmth and compassion into the learning place. Amen.**

Strength to lead

Amos 5:1–15
'Seek good, not evil, that you may live. Then the LORD God Almighty will be with you, just as you say he is. Hate evil, love good; maintain justice in the courts.' (v15)

As teachers we are all encouraged to lead. In our classrooms we lead the learning of our students. Some of us may also have a formal leadership role in terms of being a subject or phase leader; others may have greater responsibilities within the context of the school and hold a senior leadership role. Perhaps leadership comes naturally to you or maybe you need to work at it. Have you considered where your strength comes from in your leadership?

As leaders we establish the rules of our area of responsibility and how we behave in our leadership. Those rules say a great deal about ourselves and the relationships we build with staff and students. The rules we make can also construct a positive or negative learning environment. Having the strength to build the right rules, with God's help, is important.

I find it helpful to consider the words of the prophet Amos when explaining the rules of my classroom. Fewer rules mean that I can focus on the important things of creating a safe and fair learning environment for my students. Could you narrow down your rules to just a few words in a similar way to Amos?

> **Loving Lord God, help me to focus on creating a learning area where students are encouraged to hate evil, love good and strive for justice for all. You are my strength God; I cannot lay down and keep these rules without you. 'I love you, LORD, my strength' (Psa. 18:1). Amen.**

Strength to encourage

'*Gracious words are a honeycomb, sweet to the soul and healing to the bones.*' (v24)

There are a number of stages in the 'life' of a teacher. Perhaps you are training to be a teacher, or newly qualified, or maybe you've had years of experience or nearing the end of your teaching career. Whatever the stage, each one presents its own challenges, and especially in how you respond to various local and national changes in education.

It is easy to become focused on one's own individual issues in the attempt to stay on top of the many demands being made on us. All the way through my career someone has gone beyond those daily challenges to encourage me. Having the strength to go beyond the situation we find ourselves in is so important.

The writer of the book of Proverbs reminds us of the need to take time to look out for those we work with who may need some encouragement. The New Living Translation explains that kind words are 'healthy for the body'. The writer understands that we are both body and mind and that both must be cared for to ensure wholeness of health in the individual. Let this encourage you: when you encourage someone, you are *really* making a difference!

> **Heavenly Father, give us eyes to see the people we work with. Give us the discernment to reach out to those who seek encouragement. Let us not be too busy to share our knowledge or insights if someone is asking for our help. I ask this prayer through the name of Jesus. Amen.**

Strength to trust

Exodus 15:1–18

'The LORD is my strength and my defence;
he has become my salvation.' (v2)

I was on holiday recently and reminded of some choruses I had learnt in Sunday school. It is strange how; even after a number of years these words remain in the mind. One chorus extolled me to 'Trust and obey'. I reflected on these words in the context of school. As a teacher I have to trust a number of people, the learning support assistants who support me in my lessons, colleagues within my department and those in the wider school community. I also have to be trusted by those I teach to have any sort of effectiveness. I have to be trusted by the senior leadership team.

We need to have the strength to continually work at building trust, and be careful that we do not cause mistrust. Keeping our promises, doing what we say we will do, having integrity in our relationships – all help to maintain trust. The bond of trust within a school is the crucial cement that underpins and binds us together as a community.

Moreover, as Christians, we trust in Jesus. 'Trust in the LORD with all your heart and lean not on your own understanding; in all your ways submit to him, and he will make your paths straight' (Prov. 3:5–6). This trust should underpin all that we do at school.

> 'The LORD is a refuge for the oppressed,
> a stronghold in times of trouble' (Psa. 9:9).
> Heavenly Father, help keep the words of
> your psalm writer at the front of my heart.
> You provide a safe place, a refuge for
> me always; keep me from forgetting this
> wonderful gift. I ask this prayer through
> Jesus Christ our Lord. Amen.

Strength to face hostility

Isaiah 41:8–16

'I have chosen you and have not rejected
you. So do not fear, for I am with you; do
not be dismayed, for I am your God. I will
strengthen you and help you; I will uphold
you with my righteous right hand.' (vv9–10)

Schools are a partnership as we build links with
the parents and guardians of our students
and the wider community. Sometimes this
relationship is tested even in the smallest of ways.
For example, there may be a misunderstanding in
your classroom, which brings about a breakup in a
friendship, accusations of bullying or a whole host of
other events. Any of these things can so easily happen
that trigger us as teachers to respond not just to the
student but also to a very angry carer. The telephone
conversation or physical encounter with the child's
carer can very much feel like we are being tested. In
those situations how do we show our gospel values
without evangelising?

In a state secular school this is a challenge. I find
that taking time to pray a short prayer before the

difficult conversation helps me to calm down and begin to see the bigger picture. It helps me to draw strength from the Lord and becomes less about my dread and more about rebuilding relationships.

The next time you face hostility remember that God says the following and let it be your strength: 'Do not fear, for I have redeemed you; I have summoned you by name; you are mine' (Isa. 43:1).

Dear Lord, before I face challenging conversations help me to focus on what is important. Help me to find the right words so that together we can move forward to help all those involved. In Jesus' name. Amen.

Strength in weakness

'*Praise be to the* LORD, *for he has heard my cry for mercy. The* LORD *is my strength and my shield; my heart trusts in him, and he helps me.' (vv6–7)*

School can so easily consume my focus and overwhelm me with demands to meet deadlines, which are an important part of my teacher role. Sometimes teachers can feel a sense of weakness in this situation. Using the example of that all-important data trail where colleagues and students rely on the fact that the data I have provided is used and measured to ensure progress and challenge. My work has to be set and marked to the right criteria, and then feedback provided to ensure learning progress of each and every one of my students. This activity demands time and the use of the right words to encourage and motivate my students. A huge undertaking!

In these situations it is important for me to remember, when I feel especially daunted, to take the time to trust in the name of the Lord our God.

This focus for my thoughts calms and helps me channel my efforts. Prayer is my communication with God, in my thoughts and in my words and in what I do in the profound and the mundane.

> **Dear Lord God, Your Son Jesus Christ understood human weakness. He experienced weakness from the people He called friend. In His love He forgave them. Let me be encouraged by this truth when I feel overwhelmed by the demands made of me and fail to fully trust in the name of the Lord. Renew my faith and my hope, as I pray, Lord. You are my rock and my redeemer. Amen.**

Strength to praise

Psalm 81

'*Sing for joy to God our strength; shout aloud to the God of Jacob! Begin the music, strike the tambourine, play the melodious harp and lyre.*' *(vv1–2)*

We have so much to celebrate and be truly grateful for as teachers. In school we are working with young and impressionable minds and we are there to make a difference in their lives. Learning is a two-way process and we should be glad when we learn lessons from our young people and colleagues.

Many of my students love to work collaboratively on dance routines. I used to feel disparaging about the time and effort given to such rehearsing at lunch time and after school, but then I saw the parts come together as a whole in a school performance. Here was joy and happiness which transformed the individual and became their gift to us as the audience. It was praiseworthy.

We work with colleagues who lift us up when we are feeling down. There is humour and fellowship when we look around us, within and without our school community. Let the joy that we feel be evident in our interactions both in and out of school. The words of the Doxology sum up for me words of praise for our heavenly Father. Use this to lift your day and seek that strength to praise your students, your colleagues and yourself!

> **'Praise God, from whom all blessings flow;**
> **Praise him, all creatures here below;**
> **Praise him above, ye heavenly host;**
> **Praise Father, Son, and Holy Ghost. Amen.'**
> **(The Doxology)**

Making welcome

Acts 9:1–18,26–28

'*But Barnabas took him and brought him
to the apostles.' (v27)*

A ll of us have at some point been the 'new person'.
Walking into a staffroom for the first time;
arriving at a course; even standing in front
of a new class of children. We've all encountered the
feelings of apprehension and uncertainty as to exactly
how we should behave. But how do we react when we
are the established person in a room and someone
else is new or even when a person is not particularly
well liked?

In Acts 9 we read about the apostle Paul's (still called
Saul at this point) journey to Damascus. Paul had
already wreaked havoc in Jerusalem, killing followers
of Jesus or throwing them into prison. Now he was
intent on doing the same thing in Damascus; but God
had another plan! As Paul encounters Jesus his life is
changed and his time in Damascus is spent preaching
in the synagogues. Eventually the angry authorities
try to kill Paul who, in a lovely twist, is rescued by the
Christians whom he had originally come to attack!

Paul flees back to Jerusalem and runs immediately to Jesus' followers, but they are terrified by his arrival, not believing that his life had been changed. I wonder how Paul felt? Unwanted, lonely, afraid, like giving up ... What would have happened if no one had accepted him?

Paul's help comes from Barnabas who accepts him and introduces him to Jesus' followers, explaining about Paul's experiences and encouraging them to trust him. From then on Paul is accepted, welcomed and used by God in an amazing way.

Our reactions to people are so important. They can make or break a person; allowing them to feel accepted and welcome or unwanted and out of place. Let's be 'welcomers'. Whether towards new staff or children; let's look for the best and give everyone a chance.

> **Lord, You accept us as we are, with all our faults and failings. Help us to accept others in the same welcoming way. Amen.**

Acts of kindness

2 Samuel 15:13–14; 17:27–29;
19:31–33; 1 Kings 2:7

'*Barzillai ... provided for the king*'
(*2 Sam. 19:32*)

K ing David is remembered as the greatest of all the kings of Israel. His exploits in battle are well documented, but today we see a different side to this great man. We see him fleeing in fear. David's wayward son Absalom has pulled together a large army who are intent on capturing Jerusalem and declaring Absalom as king. As David receives the message that the army is marching towards Jerusalem, he gathers together his family and servants, and runs!

It seems strange that the great King David doesn't stay to fight. Maybe it is the rift in his own family that has sapped his energy; maybe the constant battles he has had to fight have left him feeling weak; maybe he is simply afraid. Whatever the reason, David can fight no longer and 2 Samuel, chapters 15 to 18, portray a sense of desperation and utter defeat. Gripped by the fear that Absalom is in hot pursuit, David is forced to lead his followers through the Jordan River in the middle of the night until they arrive exhausted, outside the city of Mahanaim. Here, at one of the lowest points in David's reign, we see the appearance of an eighty-year-old man named Barzillai who simply provides bedding, food and drink for the Israelites. This act of kindness re-energises King David, leading him to muster an army to stand against Absalom. Amazing isn't it, that such a small act could bring about such a complete change? However, is it not true that often the small, thoughtful, kind things that we have been the recipients of are the things that have made a huge difference in our lives? A thoughtful word, a meal delivered by a friend ...

Let's actively look for opportunities to be kind, and then watch to see what a difference it can make!

> **Lord, You never stop showing kindness to us. Please help us to actively seek to show Your love by the way we treat others. Amen.**

An act of protection

1 Samuel 26:1–12; 2 Samuel 21:15–17
'But Abishai son of Zeruiah came to David's rescue' (2 Sam. 21:17)

King David is probably best known for his childhood defeat of the Philistine giant, Goliath. From that point on David develops into a skilled fighter and leader until eventually he takes his place as Israel's protector and king. The books of Samuel and Chronicles are full of David's exploits in battle as he leads victorious conquests, gaining his reputation as a mighty warrior. However, today's verses show a lesser-known side to David – he is in danger and needs protection.

Abishai is the nephew of David and is listed as the commander of 'The Thirty' – David's leading soldiers. In 2 Samuel 21, David is growing old and, as he heads out for battle, he is tired (v15). As the fighting continues David becomes increasingly exhausted until he comes face to face with another Philistine, Ishbi-Benob, who is intent on killing him. In the king's moment of greatest need, Abishai leaps to David's defence and saves him. From that point on, for his own protection, David is no longer allowed to go into battle.

One of the greatest responsibilities of teaching is the protection of the children within our care. Sometimes, like Abishai we need to 'leap' to their defence or sometimes we need to be constantly at their side helping them through their 'battles of life'. Either way, we are often the only people there for them to turn to. As teachers we are in a unique position. Whether for physical or emotional protection we are on the front line, with our words and actions having the power to change lives. Sometimes the need for protection is obvious; often needs will only become apparent as we take the time and make the effort to get to know the children and gain their trust. Let's ask God to guide us as we seek to be protectors.

> **Lord, You know each one of us better than anyone else ever will do. Help us to see needs in others and to strive to be there to help. Amen.**

Giving support

Exodus 17:10–13

' *'When Moses' hands grew tired ... Aaron and Hur held his hands up – one on one side, one on the other' (v12)* '

Target setting, league tables, career advancement, promotion, status symbols ... We live in a world which encourages us to push onwards and upwards, often with little thought for those around us. So many people are motivated by the need to get ahead, to be first and to be successful. Moses is perhaps one of the best known characters in the Bible and yet in today's reading we see this great leader in need of support himself.

How do we react to those around us? How do we treat those in leadership over us? Do we look for ways to help people even if our actions will remain unseen and will receive no reward? Here we see Aaron and Hur simply fetching a stone for Moses to sit on and then carefully holding his arms until sunset – a small action with huge results. Sometimes we need to 'hold the arms' of another person. By doing so we may never receive thanks or recognition – most people have never heard of Hur! Yet our actions can have a knock-on reaction which affects many people. Aaron and Hur were not seeking praise or glory; they simply saw a need and selflessly stepped in to help.

Sometimes we can be quick to help friends or colleagues but slow to realise that those in leadership may need our support and not our criticism. As we think of those with whom we work or even of leaders within our churches, can we see those who are tired and weary and need someone to draw alongside them? The apostle Paul summed it up in Philippians 2:3–4, 'Do nothing out of selfish ambition or vain conceit. Rather, in humility value others above yourselves, not looking to your own interests but each of you to the interests of the others.'

> **Lord, help us to think of others before ourselves. Help us to look for those who are tired in the battle of life and to step in to support them in their time of need. Amen.**

The extra mile

2 Timothy 1:15–18
*'when he was in Rome, he searched hard
for me until he found me.' (v17)*

Most scholars believe that 2 Timothy is Paul's last recorded letter. The tone of the letter is certainly more solemn, as Paul states, 'I am already being poured out like a drink offering ... my departure is near. I have fought the good fight, I have finished the race' (2 Tim. 4:6–7).

During Paul's first imprisonment in Rome, he was held under house arrest where he was allowed visitors and would have been relatively comfortable. 2 Timothy is written during Paul's second imprisonment in Rome, where his circumstances were very different. Chained in dark, damp cells, Roman prisoners were dependent on family and friends to bring food and clothing and to provide basic needs. Paul is alone in prison and with Emperor Nero intent on searching out and killing the Christians, Paul wasn't receiving many visitors! Whilst throughout the letter Paul writes many encouraging words, maybe his true feelings are seen in 4:16 when he states that 'everyone deserted me'.

Imagine then how Paul must have felt when, despite the danger and shame of knowing a prisoner, Onesiphorus arrives in Rome, searches Paul out and provides for his needs! No doubt this was a dangerous action on the part of Onesiphorus but he was willing to put himself in danger for the sake of his friend Paul. In verse 18 we see that he had helped Paul many other times in the past; this time he went 'the extra mile'!

There is no doubt that Onesiphorus' reputation would suffer through his acquaintance with a prisoner. What about us? Are there people around us who need our help today? Is it 'dangerous' for our reputations to help someone unpopular, someone whom people usually avoid? Are there members of staff, children, parents, friends who need us to go the 'extra mile'?

> **Lord, we know that You are with us when we are lonely and afraid. Help us to be there for others when they face hard situations on their own. Help us to go the extra mile as we seek to point others towards You. Amen.**

Just a thought

2 Kings 4:8–17

*'Let's make a small room on the roof ...
Then he can stay there whenever he comes
to us.' (v10)*

O ver the last few days we have considered the importance of welcoming others, being kind, protecting, supporting and going the extra mile, but today's reading gives us the basis for all these other areas – thoughtfulness.

In biblical times, prophets would travel extensively as they brought God's message to the people. In many ways it must have been a lonely existence with little opportunity to make friends. Yet in this passage we see a special friendship developing between the prophet Elisha and a married couple from the town of Shunem. Firstly, Elisha is simply invited for a meal, later he visits the couple every time he returns to the area. These visits in themselves were no doubt important to the travelling prophet, but imagine Elisha's surprise when he turns up one day and finds that they have built an extension for him! I wonder what he felt like – welcomed, supported, protected, loved.

This amazing act of kindness, as these two people went 'the extra mile', must surely have changed his life. Certainly he is touched by their action. The verses that follow see Elisha seeking to return their kindness and the couple are blessed with the birth of a son!

What is it that fills our thoughts? Are we too busy to take the time to think about other people? Are we so full of ourselves and our own needs that we simply don't have enough space to see those around us who are actually in need? None of the areas we've considered this week will happen if we don't make time to think about other people and then act upon what we see. Let's ask God to help us to be thoughtful, to take action and to make a difference.

> **Lord, Psalm 139 states that your thoughts**
> **about me are too numerous to count!**
> **Thank You for the reassurance this brings.**
> **Please help me to be thoughtful towards**
> **others in everything that I say and do. Amen.**

The power of encouragement

Acts 9:19–31
'But Barnabas took [Saul] and brought him to the apostles.' (v27)

'Flatter me, and I may not believe you. Criticize me, and I may not like you … Encourage me, and I will not forget you.' So says the writer William Arthur Ward. I've certainly never forgotten Mrs Alexander, the teacher who encouraged me to succeed in a way I didn't believe possible.

The Holy Spirit, given to indwell us (John 14:16), brings us both encouragement and counsel. With His empowering, we have the possibility to encourage our pupils, by praise and exhortation, to succeed beyond the limits of their imagination. Our words are powerful and can bring life.

I once participated in a Christian training course during which only positive feedback could be given. At first it seemed false finding the one good aspect to comment on someone's very hesitant performance. But halfway through the course another participant commented, 'If this is what heaven is like, I can't wait!' The atmosphere of love, warmth and acceptance was tangible; and even the shyest, most nervous, participant grew in confidence and ability at an astounding rate.

We read today of the vital role of Barnabas (meaning 'son of encouragement', Acts 4:36), in helping to nurture the newly-converted disciple, Saul. Had Barnabas not believed Saul's story, fearlessly represented him to the apostles in Jerusalem and given his time, prayer and companionship over the coming years, would Saul have been accepted within the Jerusalem church, accomplished his amazing ministry to the Gentiles or grown to the stature of apostle? We'll never know.

> **Lord, may Your Holy Spirit speak through me to the children I teach, encouraging them to develop every aspect of the gifting You've placed within them. Amen.**

Entertaining angels unawares

Acts 12:25–13:16,42–43
'many of the Jews and devout converts to Judaism followed Paul and Barnabas, who ... urged them to continue in the grace of God.' (v43) ❜

We continue looking at Barnabas's role – firstly as Saul's mentor, encourager and friend, and then as his companion and supporter. At some point in their partnership it appears that Barnabas changed from being lead apostle to the one who supported. In Acts 13 we find Barnabas and Saul being sent out from Antioch on their mission, but later in their journey Paul takes the lead. Barnabas must surely have been overjoyed to see the growth in ability, maturity and spiritual anointing in Paul. But taking a supporting role required humility; it may not necessarily have been easy for him.

Which leads me on to my rather 'tongue in cheek' title for today. The writer of Hebrews encourages us to offer hospitality to strangers, 'for thereby some have entertained angels unawares' (13:2, AV). On first meeting the children in our class, they too are 'strangers' to us – and whilst they're not all 'little angels', we have no real idea of the hidden treasure of potential, ability and creativity within them.

I've occasionally been taken aback by how inaccurate my perceptions have been: a 'switched off' child who was, in fact, raving about my lessons at home; a teenager (whose respect I believed I'd lost) who, twenty years later, told me that just wasn't true, and refused to use my first name out of respect! We cannot know how the seeds we sow in the lives of our pupils will ultimately bear fruit – think of Anne Sullivan, the teacher of Helen Keller. Our pupils may contain within them seeds of greatness, which God has given us the privilege of nurturing – even if it will be others who will see the fruit.

> **Lord, may I see the young people I teach through Your eyes – and not limit their potential to develop in ways I could never imagine possible. Amen.**

Silence, please!

Mark 6:6–13,30–34
*'[Jesus] said to them, "Come with me
by yourselves to a quiet place and get
some rest."' (v31)*

'Silence is golden,' crooned the Tremeloes.
And it's true. But, for most teachers, silence
during a school day is a rare commodity.
Teaching languages, my days were filled with sound:
repetition, pair work, listening comprehensions and
lunchtime oral practice. In the form room, my tutor
group wanted to chat to me – and the noise in the
dinner hall was deafening! Enjoying a moment's
silence was rare indeed.

Yet it's when we're at our very busiest that
silence and solitude are most essential. As we
read today, Jesus was hounded, at times, by the
crowds and so busy that He didn't even have time
to eat. (We all know that pressure!) Yet He often
deliberately removed Himself from the busyness to
spend time in prayer with His Father, stilling His
heart to listen, refocus priorities, and receive fresh
revelation and guidance.

We too need to create 'sacred spaces' in our day: moments to pause and be silent; to re-centre on God and receive fresh empowering. Some I know (teachers included) choose to stop for a moment, reflect, then pray the Lord's prayer, at a precise time during their daily lunch hour. Finding a private spot alone to do this may be a challenge, but if all else fails there's always the loo! I remember, during one particularly busy period, God regularly telling me to sit still for an extra two minutes at lunchtime before rushing off to complete my tasks. Those two minutes of silence and stillness seemed endless – but were so refreshing.

Where can you create a 'sacred space' to meet God for a few moments during your day? You won't regret that time – however busy you are.

> **Lord, I long for moments of stillness and silence with You. Help me to find a way to re-centre my thoughts on You. Amen.**

Examination time

Psalm 139

'Search me, God, and know my heart; test me and know my anxious thoughts … and lead me in the way everlasting.' (vv23–24)

Exams, assessments, ratings and league tables can be stressful and overwhelming. A friend accurately reported that her group wasn't capable of attaining a certain level and was accused of 'letting the school down'. (Other colleagues had confided that they'd deliberately overestimated their pupils' ability.) Angry and humiliated, my friend felt like crying: a newly-qualified teacher, who also truthfully reported her group's non-attainment, *did* go home and cry. Teaching is emotionally draining. How do we manage?

As we read today, our all-seeing God knows our motives and the truth of every situation we face. He cares deeply about our hurt, our worries and our anger, and wants to bring healing. Do we let Him? I certainly never did. I critically evaluated my teaching daily, but was out of touch with my growing emotional pain.

I recently discovered the Examen, a prayer originally taught by St Ignatius. To practise it in its simplest form, ask the Holy Spirit to guide you at the end of each day as you ask yourself two questions: 1) What has brought life to me today? 2) What has drained life from me today?

In being thankful for the life-giving moments and asking God to heal those that were painful, many experience a slow healing and transformation. Our self-awareness grows. We understand more of our unique calling and become more able to forgive ourselves for our failings and imperfections, knowing we are loved – even when we get it wrong.

So, let's follow David's example in expressing our emotions to the Lord; and allow Him to restore us, spiritually and emotionally.

> **Lord, help me to bring You both my joy and pain and, as You care for me, please heal and guide me. Amen.**

Teachability

Psalm 32:8–9; Mark 4:1–20

'*The LORD says, "I will teach you the way
you should go … Don't be stupid like a
horse or a mule, which must be controlled
with a bit and bridle to make it submit."*'
(Psa. 32:8–9, GNB)

'Stubborn? Me? Never!' were almost my exact
words when I felt the Lord gently speaking
to me from the words of David's psalm we
read above. I hadn't expected the Lord to liken me
to a mule, but sensed that He was right. Yes, I was
stubborn. And He wanted to change that. Was I
willing to let Him?

How often do we moan about our more challenging
pupils – and their lack of 'teachability'? Do we, as
teachers, ever forget the fact that we too are still
being taught? How teachable are we? Do you, like me,
ever find yourself resisting the voice of God when He
highlights a particular behaviour or habit He wants
to change?

Jesus talked about 'teachability' in His parable
of the sower. He knew that some listeners would

not respond to His teaching; others would respond eagerly, but give up when the going got tough; yet others would be distracted and half-hearted; but some would be willing to open themselves to His Word and want to be changed. However, all His listeners had the same fertile 'soil' in their hearts. It was only the condition of the ground that varied.

I've discovered that, at different times in my life, my response to Jesus may vary. If I feel disappointed with God, the 'soil' of my heart tends to harden and His Word bounces off me, failing to penetrate; at other times the pressures of life (thorns) threaten to overwhelm me. Yet I thank God for the many fruitful times too. What about you? What is the Lord teaching you currently? Pray for the Holy Spirit to 'water' the soil of your heart and make His Word fruitful in and through you.

> **Lord, thank You for being my Teacher.**
> **Help me to be teachable in every area of**
> **life – and show me where I may be**
> **'turning a deaf ear' to Your voice. Amen.**

Lifelong learning

Psalm 119:97–105,169–176

*'I long for your salvation, L*ORD*, and your law gives me delight. Let me live that I may praise you, and may your laws sustain me.' (vv174–175)*

I discovered the inspiring concept of lifelong learning whilst at university. The idea of being learners for life and not just while at school seemed obvious. It matched my passion for learning new skills and my constant curiosity in the world around me. As teachers, we long to impart our own passion for learning and study to our pupils; so that their school experience is not an end in itself, but a platform from which to develop their character and abilities throughout their lives.

As a disciple of Christ, we are each called to a life of continual growth in maturity, development in gifting and transformation of character. The apostle Paul instructs us to 'continue to work out [our] salvation with fear and trembling, for it is God who works in [us]'; and 'to be transformed by the renewing of [our] mind' (Phil. 2:12–13; Rom. 12:2). Whether a Christian for forty years, or young in the faith; we each face the same challenge. Can we echo the words of the psalmist and share his passion for growing in God?

Recently hosting a Bible discovery course, I was humbled and delighted to discover the age of two delegates, 87 and 90. The couple, passionate, joyful and wise Christians, were an inspiration to us. Henry Ford's words rang true: 'Anyone who stops learning is old, whether at twenty or eighty. Anyone who keeps learning stays young.'

How are you 'staying young'? Does your year include time for you to delve further into study and exploration of your faith, as well as into your hobbies and passions? Finding that precious time may be hard, but it will be life giving.

> **Lord, I am Your disciple. Show me how I
> can deepen my knowledge and love of You.
> Amen.**

Love the Lord with all your thinking

Romans 12:1–8

'*Do not conform to the pattern of this world, but be transformed by the renewing of your mind. Then you will be able to test and approve what God's will is – his good, pleasing and perfect will.*' (v2)

Sometimes we are expected to focus on so many things that we can lose the plot. Our thoughts race with possibilities and impossibilities. How in all of this do we allow time for our thinking to be shaped and moulded by our Creator? Let us listen to God, the great thinker, provider, source of all inspiration and knowledge and wisdom. Let us be encouraged by conversations and discussion with colleagues at work. The creation account in Genesis declares that we are made in the image of God, *Imago Dei*. How fully do we use that God-given facility, our mind, to focus on growing in faith as a Christian? Let's not neglect to read our Bibles, which contain the words of God, and focus on Jesus, who is the Word. How can we as teachers live this out in our daily work with students, teachers and those we meet?

In Romans, we are invited to be transformed by the renewing of our mind so that we can fulfil God's will. Take a moment now to ponder what this means to you. Then during today, try to remember this in all your thoughts.

> **Lord, when I reflect on the marvel of your creation I am humbled by the wonder of a being who has demonstrated such creative genius through love. I struggle to comprehend the idea of creation and my part in it. You Lord have a plan for each and every one of us. Help me to learn what it is that I have to do and how it should be done. Give me the courage to accept the transforming and renewing of my mind through the love and example of Your Son, Jesus Christ. Amen.**

Think differently

Matthew 20:1–16
'*So the last will be first, and the first will be last.*' *(v16)*

I s it just a struggle to the end of the day? Are we wishing for the end of the week before it has begun? Know that your work is not just a job, it is a service with people for people and our work is also a form of worship to God. We are first people, then teachers.

Jesus taught His friends, in many ways, that they had to think differently. In many of His parables and actions He challenged them to focus on what the kingdom of God is all about.

Sometimes we can be inspired by the lives of other Christians who live out a life of faith by thinking differently. I read a book by a nun who was first involved in a remedial reading programme for the poor and marginalised in New Orleans. Later she was asked to become a pen friend for a condemned man on death row. In her naivety she agreed to become his spiritual advisor, which would entail her being a witness to his execution. This experience and other executions prompted her to write the book *Dead Man Walking*, which became a film of the same name. In the book there is a focus on the love of Jesus for all humanity. Loving the unlovely is truly different to the world's way of thinking and acting.

Into which situations can you act and think differently today?

> **Dear Lord, You know how difficult it can be sometimes to push ourselves to really use the mind that You have given us.**
> **Please prompt us to not just stretch our intellect in the solving of the mundane problems of life, but when it comes to questions of the kingdom of heaven.**
> **You Lord are a generous employer, with a different set of values to most bosses.**
> **For this we give You grateful thanks. Amen.**

Systematic thinkers

Psalm 23
' he leads me beside quiet waters …
He guides me along the right paths …
You anoint my head with oil' (vv2–3,5)

Some people have very organised minds. This is often linked to a gift in administration or a gift in teaching. When such gifts are developed and used in schools they provide order and calm and promote clarity of thinking. What a help for growing minds to have viewpoints and arguments clearly sifted as teachers present new information.

Systematic thinking can also be creative; it has often led to new ways of approaching the education of the young. We only have to look at how Early Years education has been influenced by great academic thinkers who considered the development of intellectual, physical, social and spiritual aspects and how that has impacted on our curriculum.

There are many colleagues in a school who have to be systematic thinkers as an essential part of their role. For instance, those who design the curriculum, and then create a timetable that we can deliver;

or those who have to make the finances work effectively for all parts of the school community; the exams office in secondary school, the staff who work in premises to maintain and ensure the smooth running of our school. We should pray for and be thankful for all of those involved in the smooth operation of our schools.

> **Heavenly Father, I want to thank You for all those in my school who are called upon daily to be systematic thinkers. Today I want to fully use the gifts that You have provided me with. I want to engage my students with learning that encourages them to think more clearly and thoughtfully. I want to help them to be more resilient when they face challenges in the classroom. Please give me focus, patience, humour and energy today. Amen.**

Divergent thinkers

Ephesians 4:1–16

‘ *'live a life worthy of the calling you have received ... to each one of us grace has been given as Christ apportioned it ... From him the whole body, joined and held together by every supporting ligament, grows and builds itself up in love, as each part does its work.' (vv1,7,16)* ’

There is not one way to teach or one ideal teacher type. For those with minds full of interesting ideas, which may tend to dart here and there, the routines of a school timetable are a helpful container and focus. The discipline of delivering lessons means inspiration is anchored to real time and can become an effective and encouraging ingredient to teaching. Variety in teaching styles affirms the preferences of our learners. Let us encourage ourselves and our colleagues to value different types of thinking.

As we referred to earlier this week we are all made in God's image. Let us together celebrate the diversity, the different talents and successes of our students and colleagues. Let us avoid jealousy or envy when considering the progress of individuals who have a flare for demonstrating these gifts; remembering that it is for the benefit of the students we work with. Let us keep an open mind and see what we can learn from each other as we develop our own practice.

> **Dear Lord, I give thanks for the people I work with, and the many gifts and talents they possess. I pray that I may be open to learning new lessons from my colleagues so that my teaching continues to improve. I want to serve the students in school in my role as teacher. Help me to remember that each child reflects You and is a child of God. Amen.**

The key to wisdom and knowledge

Proverbs 2

'Listen to what is wise and try to understand it. Yes, beg for knowledge; plead for insight. Look for it as hard as you would for silver or some hidden treasure. If you do, you will know what it means to fear the LORD and you will succeed in learning about God.' (vv2–5, GNB)

We are responsible for the knowledge that we have, but knowledge in itself is not wisdom. It is an interesting fact that the more you know, the more there is to know. No one person can know everything; even computers have a limit to their memory, however large mankind has tried to make it.

How to use knowledge is wisdom and the key to this treasure has not changed in thousands of years. The writer of the book of Proverbs speaks eloquently to his son of the need for wisdom – first to know the Lord and secondly to gain an understanding of righteousness and justice. As teachers we should have that love of learning and thirst for knowledge, but it is how we use it that is important. To have those insights is truly something to desire.

There are warnings of the need to keep to the straight path and there is something about this text that as teachers we can almost visualise the youngster listening and wanting to do what is right, but vulnerable and easily distracted. How can we help our students to thirst for knowledge and then use it wisely?

> **Heavenly Father, keep in our minds the wisdom shown through Your Son Jesus Christ, the great teacher. Inspire us by His example to use both our knowledge and wisdom to teach the students in our care. Amen.**

Thinking about the future

Jeremiah 29:4–14

"'I will come to you and fulfil my good promise ... For I know the plans I have for you," declares the LORD, "plans to prosper you and not to harm you, plans to give you hope and a future."' (vv10–11)

I've read that when Martin Luther, one of the key figures of the Protestant Reformation, attended school as a pupil, one of his teachers, before the lesson began, would remove his hat and bow before his students acknowledging their future roles and importance in society. The act was symbolic but it must have made a powerful impression as it was recalled by these young men in later life.

As teachers we may have that opportunity to lead an assembly. As you look out at your students don't see them at the age they are, but consider what they might become in the future. Perhaps politicians, nurses, entrepreneurs, musicians, mechanics, actors and so on. Each one has an amazing future and we as teachers can be part of that and make a difference in their lives.

When we meet with our students let us remember that each and every one reflects an aspect of God and inspire us to show the same courtesy and respect to every child of our Father. Our trust is in the Lord for our future relationships with all those we work with, be they students, staff or visitors to our schools.

> **Dear Lord, help me to keep a healthy respect for the students I teach. Help me to help them develop their full potential through my encouragement and support. Help me to recognise that their dependence must be replaced by independence as they mature. Amen.**

The protector

Exodus 2:1–10; 15:2

'The LORD is my strength and my defence;
he has become my salvation.' (15:2)

Despite their status as slaves in Egypt and the cruel treatment they received, the people of Israel multiplied to the extent that Pharaoh became worried. Afraid that the Israelites would soon outnumber the Egyptians, Pharaoh made the terrible decree that all male babies must be killed. When Jochebed discovered that she was pregnant we can only imagine her fear as the birth approached. When baby Moses arrives on the scene he is hidden for as long as possible before being placed in the basket on the River Nile. It appears that Jochebed herself prepares the basket and places it in the reeds; but it is Moses' sister who keeps watch to see what happens to her baby brother.

As the story unfolds a beautiful twist ensures that Jochebed is able to nurse Moses for the first few years of his life, using those precious years to teach him the Israelites' history and unknowingly preparing him for his future work. But what if Miriam had not been willing to keep watch? What if she had been too afraid to speak to Pharaoh's daughter? What if she had not run to fetch her mother and introduce her as a possible nurse for baby Moses? Moses' life would have been very different if his sister had not been there to watch and protect him.

In the same way that Miriam was given the massive responsibility of protecting her brother, many of the children in our classes have enormous responsibilities at home, caring for parents and other siblings or even working to provide much needed finance. While we may struggle in class with their tired faces and lack of attention, we must realise that they are coping with huge pressures. It is easy to criticise but often these children are in great need of our care and support.

> **Lord, help me to see each child through Your eyes. Help me understand their needs and concerns. Help me to love more than criticise. Amen.**

The sharer

John 6:1–15

'*Here is a boy with five small barley loaves and two small fish, but how far will they go among so many?' (v9)*

The feeding of the 5,000 is perhaps one of the best known stories in the Bible. In fact, other than Jesus' resurrection, it is the only miracle recorded in all four of the Gospels. At the end of a hard day's teaching, Jesus takes a small amount of food, gives thanks and miraculously feeds more than 5,000 hungry mouths and, to top it all, there are twelve basketfuls left over!

In Mark's account we read that initially Jesus tells the disciples to feed the crowds (Mark 6:37). As they look at him in horror, Philip makes the statement that it 'would take more than half a year's wages' to give each person even one mouthful! The situation seems hopeless, until the action of a small boy changes everything. I find this little boy fascinating. Having seen many children desperate for dinnertime to arrive, I find it amazing that this little boy hasn't finished his food long before now! Even more amazing is that he is willing to share it!

I can almost see the battle going on within him – shall I offer it to Jesus ... shall I eat it myself?

His decision to hand what he has to Jesus leads to an amazing miracle – what must this little boy have felt like when he saw what happened!

As teachers we all know children who may struggle academically but who have other qualities that shine from them. Maybe they are kind, good at making friends, thoughtful, peacemakers or simply like this boy – good at sharing! Possibly our most important role is to look for these qualities in children and help them develop these gifts, recognising their importance in every part of our lives. Likewise we need to be offering all our own gifts and abilities to God. Who knows what God can do with something small that we offer to Him!

> **Lord, You have made each one of us different and special. Please use all the abilities You have given to us and help us to seek opportunities to pull out the best in those around us. Amen.**

The bold speaker

2 Kings 5:1–15

*'and his flesh was restored and became
clean like that of a young boy.' (v14)*

Whether the servant girl in this story was taken captive by Naaman himself during one of the raids he led into neighbouring Israel or whether she was bought by the household from the slave market, we are not told. What we do know is that this young girl is many miles from home in a foreign country, serving the wife of army commander Naaman. Everything appears wonderful for this highly respected soldier until he catches leprosy; a dreaded disease which often meant sufferers had to live outside the city walls. As this servant girls sees the family struck with the horror of this terrible news she realises that she could help.

Let's imagine ourselves in that situation. We are slaves in a foreign country, taken against our will, not expected to have an opinion or even to speak to our owners. Would we dare to speak out? Would we want to? There must have been many mixed feelings as this child approaches her mistress and begins

134

to speak. Maybe it is sheer desperation that makes Naaman and his wife take notice of a slave girl, or maybe they have seen something different in her attitude that points towards the reality of her belief in God. Whatever the reason, Naaman follows her advice and the result is healing.

All of us have outspoken children in our classes; children who are not afraid to stand up for their point of view. Sometimes these children can be challenging and hard to handle but, with the correct help and guidance, these could be the people who will, in the future, stand up for what is right and be unafraid to speak out in defence of those in need. Let's encourage and guide these children as we look for their potential.

> **Lord, help us to be bold in standing up for You and for what is right. Help us as we encourage our children to do the same. Amen.**

The friendship maker

1 Samuel 20

‘*because he loved him as he loved himself.*’
(v17)

Friends matter! Even if we are famous, successful and have ample material possessions, most of us still want and need friends. Muhammad Ali once said, 'Friendship is the hardest thing in the world to explain. It's not something you learn in school. But if you haven't learned the meaning of friendship, you really haven't learned anything.'

Today we see the depth of the friendship between Jonathan, the son of King Saul, and David, the future king. As David shares his fear that Saul is about to kill him, Jonathan, despite his disbelief, swears his allegiance to protect David forever. Together they hatch a plan of escape should David's fears be correct. When Jonathan realises that King Saul is indeed trying to kill David, he springs into action and saves David's life. In a moving scene the two men weep as they say goodbye (v41), knowing that it may be a long time before they meet again.

David and Jonathan must have known each other as boys, when David would visit the palace to calm King Saul by playing his lyre (1 Sam. 16:19–23). We don't know exactly when they first met but we do know that they were still boys when their friendship began to take root. Just after David had killed Goliath we are told that David and Jonathan became 'one in spirit' (1 Sam. 18:1).

How important are our friends? Do we make time for them? In the busyness of life, so often the things that really matter are overlooked as we concentrate on matters of lesser importance. Do our friends know that they are important to us?

Some children have a great ability to make friends while others struggle. As teachers we have the wonderful opportunity to help children in this area – an area which is essential for their future happiness.

> **Lord, You are our greatest friend. 'Greater love has no one than this: to lay down one's life for one's friends' (John 15:13). Help us to live in the light of this. Amen.**

The action taker

> **2 Chronicles 34:1–8**
> *'He did what was right in the eyes of the
> LORD ... not turning aside to the right or
> to the left.' (v2)*

As Josiah sat on his throne, having been
crowned King of Israel, many thoughts must
have flooded his mind. His father, King
Amon, had just been killed by the palace officials.
In reaction to this the Israelites had killed the palace
officials before proclaiming Josiah the king. For an
eight-year-old boy the task ahead must have seemed
unwanted and daunting!

We know nothing of the first eight years of
Josiah's reign but at the age of sixteen (v3), we read
that he began to seek God. From this point on Josiah
begins to take responsibility and to take action. He
gets rid of all the altars built for the worship of false
gods before moving on to repairing the neglected
temple. From here he re-introduces the people to the
Book of the Law, given to Moses, before reinstating
the Passover celebration. Throughout his reign he is
seen to do 'what was right in the eyes of the LORD' –

what a statement about someone who was thrust into such a position at such a young age – no resentment, no complaining.

We've all come across children who always seem to be at the forefront of every situation. If people have an argument/fight, they are there trying to sort it out. If something appears unjust, they are the first to point it out! They are often reactionary, often impulsive, always questioning and sometimes hard work to have around! They are not the children who sit quietly in the classroom! However, what potential these children have if they are moulded and guided in the right direction. What leaders they could become! As teachers we have the amazing privilege of being involved in helping develop these children's God-given gifts. Let's pray that the children in our care begin to seek God in the same way as King Josiah.

> **Lord, You have made us all to be different.**
> **Help us to see the good in every child.**
> **Amen.**

The listener

1 Samuel 3

' *'Speak, for your servant is listening.' (v10)* '

From the moment of his conception Samuel was a special child. His mother Hannah had spent years suffering the cruel jibes of Elkanah's other wife concerning her inability to have children. Eventually Hannah makes a vow that if she were to bear a son she would give him back to God for all the days of his life (1 Sam. 1:11). When God answers Hannah's prayer she is true to her promise and, as a young boy, Samuel is left at the temple under the care of Eli the priest.

The comment that, 'In those days the word of the LORD was rare' (v1), makes it clear that Samuel will never have experienced God speaking to him before. Indeed when God speaks to Samuel he runs to Eli assuming that he has called him. On Eli's instructions, the third time God calls to him, Samuel utters the well-known words, 'Speak, for your servant is listening'. This is the start of a lifetime in which Samuel is constantly listening to God and following His directions.

Whilst Samuel's willingness to listen to God is key to the passage, it is also Samuel's eagerness to run to Eli's side, which is beautiful to observe. Verse 4 conjures up the picture of a young boy, leaping out of bed and running to find out what an old man needs. It seems that Samuel was a good listener to other people as well as to God – a talent which continued throughout Samuel's life.

In our classes we have children who may always struggle with academic demands but who have the wonderful gift of being a good listener and carer. What a privilege to encourage these children and to help others learn from their special skills. We should never underestimate these children – in the future they are the sort of people we will want to be around!

> **Lord, help us not to be so full of our own ideas and needs that we fail to listen to those around us. Amen.**

Called

Hebrews 11:8–10

' *'By faith Abraham, when called to go to a place he would later receive as his inheritance, obeyed and went' (v8)* '

D own through the ages, the idea of a journey as a metaphor for our lives has been popular, from Chaucer's *Canterbury Tales* to Bunyan's *Pilgrim's Progress* and even the film of our childhood, *The Wizard of Oz*. In recent times there has been a renewed interest in the idea of pilgrimage – the 2010 film, *The Way*, starring Martin Sheen set on the Camino Compostela in Spain, and several television travel documentaries focusing on the theme, visiting sacred or holy places of pilgrimage. It is an old metaphor that has stood the test of time.

Over the next few days we're going to be looking at this idea, reflecting on our own lives, particularly in the light of Abraham's journey described in Hebrews 11. We'll consider what to expect from the journey, how we travel with others and where we are going.

So, where does the journey begin?

Well, quite simply, it begins with God. In these

verses from Hebrews, Abraham's journey begins with God calling him to leave his old home, Ur, because God intends to make him into a great nation and to be a blessing (Gen. 12:1–2).

When Jesus begins His public ministry, God the Father affirms that He has been called and chosen: 'This is my Son, whom I love; with him I am well pleased' (Matt. 3:17).

Jesus calls us as He called His disciples: 'Come, follow me' (Matt. 4:19).

We have been called to follow Jesus. It all starts with God; He is the one who has initiated our journey with Him. Let's give thanks to Him for that today.

> **Lord, thank You that You love me and**
> **that You have called me to a life with You.**
> **Thank You that You initiated my journey and**
> **that along with Jesus at His baptism, I know**
> **that I am Your beloved. Amen.**

Loved and chosen

Ephesians 1:3–14

'*For he chose us in him before the creation of the world to be holy and blameless in his sight. In love he predestined us for adoption to sonship through Jesus Christ, in accordance with his pleasure and will*'
(vv4–5)

Today we're going to linger a little longer, thinking about the call to follow God.

These words written by Paul to the Ephesians seem to tumble onto the page, with one incredible thought after another. It looks like lofty theology at first glance and yet at its heart it is so simple – God loves us, has chosen us and has great purposes involving us.

Our lives are not an accident and neither is the call to follow Jesus. Sometimes we might wonder why God chose us and what He can possibly do with our little and imperfect lives – but these verses are attempting to express the glory and the grace of God's ways. This is exactly what He loves to do – to choose the little and the unimportant to love

Him and journey with Him and to be involved in His work on earth. Sometimes we have a hard time grasping this.

It might be helpful to reread the verses again slowly, saying aloud words and phrases like, 'blessed', 'chosen', 'in love'. Allow them to speak deeply to you.

One of the greatest gifts that we can bring as teachers is our assurance that we are loved, chosen and called by God. When we have that sense of value ourselves, our lives convey it to those around us. We begin to see others as 'loved and chosen' by God. They may not have responded to His call yet, but that doesn't change God's total love for them.

> **Lord, these words about being loved,**
> **called and chosen are just so incredible.**
> **I want them not to be just theology in my**
> **head, but truths in my heart that affect my**
> **life and the way I see others too. Amen.**

Where, oh where, are we going?

Hebrews 11:8–10
'By faith Abraham, when called to go to a place he would later receive as his inheritance, obeyed and went, even though he did not know where he was going.' (v8)

Abraham's response to God's call was very simple – he 'obeyed and went'. He believed God and he left his home and began his journey with God. And then the most intriguing part – 'even though he did not know where he was going'.

For some of us, the idea of not knowing where we are going is an exhilarating idea and we would love to be on an adventure with an unknown destination every day. For others of us, that's not the case; we like to know where we are going and we plan and prepare, eliminating the unknowns.

In our work we must plan – following programmes of study and setting attainment targets. We make sure that the students know where every lesson is heading and what they will have learned by the end.

Often we have also planned out our career path, knowing exactly where we want to be in ten years time. And those in positions of leadership must lead with vision, confidence and clarity.

But we must take notice of this most profound teaching about faith. The clue is to read right to the end of these verses. Abraham was called by God to go to a place prepared by God. He did know his destination, but not what the pathway was going to be like to get there. He set his 'sat nav' to 'city of God' and set off.

This is God's way – to lead us, step by step, walking beside us and teaching us to trust and to follow. And sometimes we need to leave our own plans behind.

> **Lord, there are times when I really don't**
> **think I know where I'm going, like Abraham.**
> **Keep me trusting in You. Amen.**

Journeying on

It is well worth taking time over this well-known psalm, for it is a psalm that takes us on a journey. God is our shepherd who leads us in verdant pastures, places of restoration and refreshment. Beautiful places. The mood shifts as we travel with Him through 'the valley of the shadow of death', a dark and threatening place. But He is close by. Enemies still lurk, but we are welcomed as honoured guests to God's table to live with Him for ever.

This describes our journey with God – taken by all who follow Him. Taken by Abraham, and you and me. Journeys with high and low points, times of darkness, loss and death, moments of joy, feasting and rest, and seasons of strife and conflict. This is the journey that shapes us – forming character and faith.

And we don't walk alone on this journey. Like a caravan travelling through the desert, we travel with others who are going in the same direction.

In our work, we have the privilege of walking alongside our students for a part of their journey. We accompany them as God accompanies us. It may be for a short while, maybe just for a year, maybe longer. We get to know them, recognise their talents and help to grow their gifts; we watch over them pastorally, we try to help those who struggle. Those in leadership have the added responsibility of walking alongside their colleagues on this path.

Let's pay attention today to the people we accompany – where on the journey are they? And how can we best walk beside them?

> **Lord, open my eyes today to those I journey alongside. Make me aware of where they are on the journey. Teach me how to be a good travelling companion. Amen.**

Unlikely treasures along the way

Matthew 13:44–46

'The kingdom of heaven is like treasure hidden in a field.' (v44)

Today I want to tell you about one of my students with whom I journeyed for a while.

Stacey was a likable ten-year-old who had a difficult home background. She and her siblings arrived an hour before school, having had no breakfast. Reading, writing, maths didn't interest her. Her usual response to such activities was a non-violent, passive resistance, but on occasion she would have angry outbursts, which often involved ripped books, tears, a dented radiator and time out.

What Stacey did love was Art, and not only did she enjoy it, but she was immensely gifted. Drawing, painting and craft drew her into another world and would keep her engrossed all day. And she produced beautiful work. It brought her immense pleasure. When anyone commented on her lovely work, she would shrug her shoulders, hardly able to receive a compliment at all. She just didn't think she was any good at anything.

I left the school just as Stacey was going to secondary school, so I don't know what happened to her. I'd like to think that she flourished as her artistic gift was recognised, but sadly I'm almost sure that she probably failed within the school system.

This is not an unusual story – there must be hundreds of 'Staceys' in our schools. But she spoke something deep into my life – she made me question my classroom practice, she challenged me about what was really important, she spoke to me about the treasure hidden in our students, and also about broken lives and the possibility of wholeness in God. She certainly deepened my prayer life. In many ways, Stacey was my teacher on the journey.

> **Lord, sometimes the roles in class are reversed and we learn more from our students than they do from us. Keep me humble and learning, and enable me to see treasure in the dark places. And bless my students today. Amen.**

Our destination

Revelation 21:1–7
'*I heard a loud voice from the throne saying,
"Look! God's dwelling-place is now among
the people, and he will dwell with them."*'
(*v3*)

And so we come to the end of our 'journeying'. We have seen that there is a definite beginning to our journey – when God calls us. This is a call to walk in His purposes, which was born out of love. In the case of Abraham, God gave him some detail – He was leading him to a particular place to become a great nation and to be a blessing. However, Abraham still had to learn to walk by faith, not knowing 'where he was going' (Heb. 11:8).

Then, we saw how and where God leads us in Psalm 23: not a continual upward journey without troubles or loss, but through different landscapes – restful, restorative, peaceful, shadowy, hazardous – leading eventually to a banquet prepared by God Himself and to His very dwelling place.

We also thought about the people we travel with and how we accompany them, whilst at the same time learning from them. We thought about how even though lives may intersect for just a little while, these are significant moments when lessons are learned and characters are strengthened.

And what a wonderful destination: 'an unseen city with real, eternal foundations—the City designed and built by God' (Heb. 11:10, *The Message*). And what a promise: 'I will dwell in the house of the LORD for ever' (Psa. 23:6).

You might like to end these twelve weeks by mapping your own journey so far. The high and low points, the people you have walked with, the significant moments, the significant people. Bring your journey to God in prayer, thanking Him for the way He has led you and trusting Him for the future.

'The Spirit and the bride say, "Come!"' (Rev. 22:17).

'"Come, follow me," Jesus said' (Matt. 4:19).

> **Lord, thank You for Your presence in my life up to this very moment. Lead me on, I pray, until I meet with You face to face. Amen.**

NATIONAL DISTRIBUTORS

UK: (and countries not listed below)

CWR, Waverley Abbey House, Waverley Lane, Farnham, Surrey GU9 8EP.

Tel: (01252) 784700 Outside UK (44) 1252 784700 Email: mail@cwr.org.uk

AUSTRALIA: KI Entertainment, Unit 21 317-321 Woodpark Road, Smithfield, New South Wales 2164 Tel: 1 800 850 777 Fax: 02 9604 3699
Email: sales@kientertainment.com.au

CANADA: David C Cook Distribution Canada, PO Box 98, 55 Woodslee Avenue, Paris, Ontario N3L 3E5
Tel: 1800 263 2664 Email: joy.kearley@davidccook.ca

GHANA: Challenge Enterprises of Ghana, PO Box 5723, Accra
Tel: (021) 222437/223249 Fax: (021) 226227 Email: ceg@africaonline.com.gh

HONG KONG: Cross Communications Ltd, 11/F Ko's House, 577 Nathan Road, Kowloon
Tel: 2780 1188 Fax: 2770 6229 Email: cross@crosshk.com

INDIA: Crystal Communications, Plot No. 125, Road No. 7, T.M.C, Mahendra Hills, East Marredpally, Secunderabad - 500026
Tel/Fax: (040) 27737145 Email: crystal_edwj@rediffmail.com

KENYA: Keswick Books and Gifts Ltd, PO Box 10242-00400, Nairobi Tel: (020) 2226047/312639 Email: sales.keswick@africaonline.co.ke

MALAYSIA: Canaanland Distributors Sdn Bhd, No. 25 Jalan PJU 1A/41B, NZX Commercial Centre, Ara Jaya, 47301 Petaling Jaya, Selangor
Tel: (03) 7885 0540/1/2 Fax: (03) 7885 0545 Email: info@canaanland.com.my

Salvation Publishing & Distribution Sdn Bhd, 23 Jalan SS 2/64, 47300 Petaling Jaya, Selangor Tel: (03) 78766411/78766797
Fax: (03) 78757066/78756360 Email: info@salvationbookcentre.com

NEW ZEALAND: KI Entertainment, Unit 21 317-321 Woodpark Road, Smithfield, New South Wales 2164, Australia
Tel: 0 800 850 777 Fax: +612 9604 3699 Email: sales@kientertainment.com.au

NIGERIA: FBFM, Helen Baugh House, 96 St Finbarr's College Road, Akoka, Lagos
Tel: (+234) 01-7747429, 08075201777, 08186337699, 08154453905
Email: fbfm_1@yahoo.com

PHILIPPINES: OMF Literature Inc, 776 Boni Avenue, Mandaluyong City
Tel: (02) 531 2183 Fax: (02) 531 1960 Email: gloadlaon@omflit.com

SINGAPORE: Alby Commercial Enterprises Pte Ltd, 95 Kallang Avenue #04-00, AIS Industrial Building, 339420
Tel: (+65) 629 27238 Fax: (+65) 629 27235 Email: marketing@alby.com.sg

SOUTH AFRICA: Life Media & Distribution, Unit 20, Tungesten Industrial Park, 7 C R Swart Drive, Strydompark 2125 Tel: (+27) 0117924277
Fax: (+27) 0117924512 Email: orders@lifemedia.co.za

SRI LANKA: Christombu Publications (Pvt) Ltd, Bartleet House, 65 Braybrooke Place, Colombo 2
Tel: (+941) 2421073/2447665 Email: christombupublications@gmail.com

USA: David C Cook Distribution Canada, PO Box 98, 55 Woodslee Avenue, Paris, Ontario N3L 3E5, Canada
Tel: 1800 263 2664 Email: joy.kearley@davidccook.ca

CWR is a Registered Charity – Number 294387

CWR is a Limited Company registered in England – Registration Number 1990308

Daily encouragement from God's Word.

Our compact, daily Bible reading notes for adults are published bimonthly and offer a focus for every need. They are available as individual issues or annual subscriptions, in print, in eBook format or by email.

Every Day with Jesus

With around half a million readers, this insightful devotional by Selwyn Hughes is one of the most popular daily Bible reading tools in the world. A large-print edition is also available.
72-page booklets, 120x170mm

Inspiring Women Every Day

Written by women for women to inspire, encourage and strengthen.
64-page booklets, 120x170mm

Life Every Day

Apply the Bible to life each day with these challenging life-application notes written by international speaker and well-known author Jeff Lucas.
64-page booklets, 120x170mm

Cover to Cover Every Day

Study one Old Testament and one New Testament book in depth with each issue, and a psalm every weekend. Two well-known Bible scholars each contribute a month's series of daily Bible studies. Covers every book of the Bible in five years.
64-page booklets, 120x170mm

For current price and to order visit **www.cwr.org.uk/subscriptions**
Also available online or from Christian bookshops

Insight series

**Handling issues that are feared,
ignored or misunderstood.**

COURSES

These invaluable teaching
days are designed both for
those who would like to
come for their own benefit
and for those who seek
to support people facing
particular issues.

For the latest course information
and dates about CWR's one-day
Insight seminars visit
www.cwr.org.uk/insightdays

BOOKS

Insight into Adult and Child bullying
by Helena Wilkinson
ISBN: 978-1-85345-912-2

Insight into Self-Esteem
by Chris Ledger and Wendy Bray
ISBN: 978-1-85345-663-3

Insight into Depression
by Chris Ledger and Wendy Bray
ISBN: 978-1-85345-538-4

Insight into Stress
by Beverley Shepherd
ISBN: 978-1-85345-790-6

 ALSO AVAILABLE AS EBOOK/KINDLE

For a complete list of the 16 titles
available in this series visit
www.cwr.org.uk/insight
Available online or from
Christian bookshops.

WAVERLEY ABBEY
COLLEGE

Learning for *life*

Our vision is to see thousands of Christian learners walk through our doors, be transformed by God's Word, and live out their new learning in their workplace.

Enrol Now

Waverley Abbey College offers a range of programmes for those wanting to find out about counselling. From one-week introductory courses to our BA and MA programmes.

New for 2015

We are hoping to introduce a range of programmes for education professionals and church leaders, starting in 2015. Keep an eye on the website for more details.

University of Roehampton
London

Counselling accredited programmes lead to awards validated by The University of Roehampton.

Open Days

Why not come along to one of our open days?
Contact us using the details below to find out more.

Please call **01252 784731** or email **registry@waverleyabbeycollege.ac.uk**
www.waverleyabbeycollege.ac.uk

Waverley Abbey College is the
Education Division of CWR **CWR**

Registered Charity No 294387 Company Registration No 1990308 CWR, Waverley Abbey House, Waverley Lane, Farnham, GU9 8EP.

Courses and seminars

Publishing and media

Conference facilities

Transforming lives

CWR's vision is to enable people to experience
personal transformation through applying God's Word
to their lives and relationships.

Our Bible-based training and resources help people
around the world to:
• Grow in their walk with God
• Understand and apply Scripture to their lives
• Resource themselves and their church
• Develop pastoral care and counselling skills
• Train for leadership
• Strengthen relationships, marriage and family life
and much more.

Our insightful writers provide daily Bible-reading
notes and other resources for all ages, and our
experienced course designers and presenters have
gained an international reputation for excellence and
effectiveness.

CWR's Training and Conference Centres in Surrey
and East Sussex, England, provide excellent facilities
in idyllic settings – ideal for both learning and spiritual
refreshment.

CWR Applying God's Word
to everyday life and relationships

CWR, Waverley Abbey House,
Waverley Lane, Farnham,
Surrey GU9 8EP, UK

Telephone: +44 (0)1252 784700
Email: info@cwr.org.uk
Website: www.cwr.org.uk

Registered Charity No 294387
Company Registration No 1990308